Ron Kramer

That's Just Kramer

From Michigan Legend
to Lombardi's "12th Man"

Ron Kramer

with

Dan Ewald

SPORTS
MEDIA
GROUP

SPORTS MEDIA GROUP

All inquiries should be addressed to:

Sports Media Group
An imprint of Ann Arbor Media Group LLC
2500 S. State Street
Ann Arbor, MI 48104

11 10 09 08 07   1 2 3 4 5

ISBN 13: 978-1-58726-433-7
ISBN 10: 1-58726-433-1

Printed and bound in the United States of America.

Library of Congress Cataloging-in-Publication Data

Kramer, Ron, 1935-
  That's just Kramer : from Michigan legend to Lombardi's "12th man" / Ron Kramer with Dan Ewald.
     p. cm.
  ISBN-13: 978-1-58726-433-7 (hardcover : alk. paper)
  ISBN-10: 1-58726-433-1 (hardcover : alk. paper) 1. Kramer, Ron, 1935- 2. Football players--United States--Biography. 3. Green Bay Packers (Football team) I. Ewald, Dan. II. Title.

GV939.K72A3 2007
796.332092--dc22
[B]

2006101808

Without the wisdom and will you so generously shared, none of this could have happened. Thanks Mom, Dad, and our entire family.

—Ron Kramer

Contents

Introduction

The basics of the games we love don't change ... only the people in them do.

The players. The owners. The businessmen who run the games. All of them look so similar to those who went before.

Missing, however, are those disarming, colorful characters that speckled sports and spiked romance into the games before the big-bucks explosion now at least a few decades old.

Professional football, baseball, and basketball franchises are now as much a part of corporate America as any major brand-name company. Owners are driven more by ledger sheets than by quality of play on the field. The men hired to produce those healthy ledger sheets had better make those numbers sing or the line of prospects waiting for a shot at big-time sports suddenly becomes one man shorter.

There was a time when the average working man could afford to treat his whole family to a game without surrendering an entire week's wages. Now, with suites and costly premium seating sprinkled throughout all new parks, the corporate customer is the preferred target for relentless ticket sellers.

While the basics on the field remain generally the same, it's impossible for players to remain immune to the effects of million dollar bingo. How else can one explain subs turning into millionaires set for life, even if they don't play?

The chase for the big bucks, at times, has nudged individual performance ahead of team play. And the lure of fairy-tale wealth has changed the essence of the individual.

There was a time, though, when players bigger than life had incomes that more closely resembled those of their next-door neighbors.

And doesn't it seem as if they had more fun?

Today's athletes certainly are bigger, stronger, and quicker than their predecessors from a less technological time. Many observers who have bridged that gap, however, question the price the transition has exacted.

No one can tell for sure when the quality of performance in any particular era was superior to that in others. Even the most casual fan, however, needs no one to tell him that the storybook players of yesterday are as extinct as black-and-white TV.

They were guys who played hard and lived as hard as they played. They were hardly different from their forty-hours-a-week working neighbors. And they remained as touchable as the guy next door.

More than thirty years ago, I was a beat writer covering a Detroit Tigers team that featured Norm Cash at first base. Cash won a batting title in 1961 and had a knack for delivering late-inning home runs to snatch victory from defeat.

Cash was a better-than-average big-league player, but was more popular for his off-field personality than anything he did on the diamond.

Gates Brown, himself a Tiger icon who signed a contract after serving time in an Ohio prison, captured the essence of Cash's popularity.

"He's the only man I ever knew who could show up at the park healthy, hurt, or hungover and still play every game like it might be his last," Brown said. "You couldn't keep him out of the lineup. You had to love him. He was so much fun to be around."

Cash was likely to show up anywhere. Even in a shot and beer bar, sitting on a stool next to a factory worker who was wearing a flannel after putting in eight hours on the job.

Cash was a poster boy for the sports character who bridged the gap between the sports star and the guy that sits in the bleachers.

True sports characters have a gift for being hilariously human. They have the same problems as the guy next door. They like to laugh, and they love to see the next guy smile. They just happen to be a sliver of that tiny brotherhood of athletes who can play a little boy's game better than almost anyone else in the world.

Ron Kramer was that kind of character. He lived large in all aspects of life. On the field. Off the field. And with his family and friends.

Stories about his insatiable appetite for life remain legendary.

Even when a pair of tickets to a Green Bay Packers' game didn't cripple the kids' college savings fund, he never cheated a fan out of a penny.

It's impossible to empirically determine the purest athlete from a state, a city, or even a particular team. If, however, the purest athlete is determined by how much an individual dominates a number of sports, the state of Michigan has produced none better than Ron Kramer—All-City, All-State, All-American, and All Pro.

And not just in one sport!

From snagging footballs to pitching pennies against a wall, Kramer was better than anyone brave enough to challenge him. Some say he was naturally gifted. Without a doubt, the talent was there. Kramer, however, lifted it to another level through an unforgiving work ethic and the discipline of a Marine drill sergeant.

His athletic career borders on the make-believe. Yet he still found time to enjoy life as an ordinary person and never had a problem skipping through the upper, middle, and lower strata of society.

Kramer still lives every day as if twenty-four hours are nothing more than the first half.

Paying the physical price for a career in the violent world of professional football, Kramer moves a little slower, but never complains about the beatings his body endured. His eyes still sparkle with that unmistakable look of a champion. He clings to a boyish wonder at the world with the same firm grip he had when he graduated from the University of Michigan a half-century ago.

While most experts concur Kramer is the purest athlete ever to grow up in the state of Michigan, it really doesn't matter. His greatest gift was to share his colorful life with sports fans everywhere.

I respect athletes who make the most of their God-given talent. I absolutely admire those who take that talent to another level through discipline and a tireless work ethic. And I cherish those who do all that while living on the edge of life and making us smile.

I miss that breed of romantic roustabout. So do sports and their new gray world of high finances.

Ron Kramer has never forgotten where he came from. Many fans won't forget the good times he shared.

Thanks, Ron.

Dan Ewald

1   *"Kramer ... It's Kramer"*

Each morning when home, Ron Kramer wakes to a recording of his own voice installed into the alarm clock next to his bed. The message is simple. Straight to the point.

"It's time to get up, Kramer," the calm voice says bluntly. "Make your bed. Adjust your attitude. And don't forget to watch your damn language."

Not too many people are greeted to a new day by the sound of their own voice. But in the world according to Ron Kramer, it's a subtle start on the bigger picture.

And it all makes sense.

"Preparation," he explains, "makes you ready to meet any challenge. When you make your bed, you've already accomplished something. Might be small. Might seem insignificant. But you're showing yourself you're prepared to deal with the really big things."

What they may be doesn't matter. Without discipline, they can't be controlled.

Discipline, he is emphatic, is the mother of attitude. It's the force that makes preparation work.

"Discipline shows how much we expect of ourselves," he echoes the lesson that was instilled into him by his parents then punctuated by one of the most demanding and celebrated coaches in the history of professional sports.

Kramer was shaped into the Vince Lombardi mold long before the pair had even met.

"Some people think all the discipline came from Lombardi," Kramer said. "A lot of it did. The same can be said for [college coach] Bennie Oosterbaan and [high school coach] Al Asbury. No one taught me more about discipline, though, than my parents."

No other single lesson did more to shape his life.

"How much are we willing to give to succeed?" Kramer asks, sounding more like Lombardi than the relentlessly ferocious player he was. "We all have an attitude. Sometimes it's good … upbeat and confident. There are times, though, when maybe we're angry. Sometimes scared or maybe feeling sorry for ourselves. How are you going to beat anything if you don't adjust your attitude?"

Then he chuckles at himself.

"That part about language?" he asks. "What the hell … sometimes I have to work on that, too."

Preparation and discipline. Kramer savors the words as much as Emeril does a freshly created delicacy. Coupled with "family, friends, team, and winning," the words define his life.

"And Freud, too," he cracks. "I'm a big-time Freudian. I think my id and ego and superego are wrapped around sex. Ol' Sigmund is my man."

Ron Kramer's life—compared even to other professional athletes—is at least a dozen degrees beyond the boundaries of the norm. Compared to the general public, it's about as normal as a weekend getaway to Baghdad.

The lives of many professional athletes bend a bit toward the bizarre. But there's only one Ron Kramer. And the athlete he represents has, for the most part, become an extinct breed.

Kramer is that colorful character who left indelible marks on the games that he played while living a life that should have come with a warning label.

"I don't mean to sound like I'm living in the past, but today's athletes are a total pain in the butt," remarked distinguished retired journalist Dave Diles.

In a meteoric career that saw him rise to the pinnacle of television sports journalism, Diles covered two years of Kramer's playing time at the University of Michigan as a writer for the Associated Press. He also is the author of several critically acclaimed sports books.

"Ron Kramer possessed all the qualities that we mourn the loss of in today's athletes," he said.

Even today at 72, Kramer's life is as conventional as political bipartisan unanimity. He's a maverick who sets his own standards. Principle, more than rules, defines precisely what those standards are.

His appetite for life is insatiable. He attacks each unfolding day with the ferocity he patented for each play of his distinguished football career. Regrets are for losers. There's no time for looking into the rearview mirror.

"Couldda ... shouldda ... wouldda," Kramer bristles at the mention of such words. "In sports, in business and life in general, you have to make a decision that applies to the present. You can't worry about what happened five years ago or what's going to happen five years from now. Make a decision, move on, and don't look back."

Kramer treasures memories from his storied past. He also acknowledges mistakes he made along the way. He prefers, however, to live in the present, leaving past and future to take care of themselves.

"Isn't life supposed to be enjoyed?" he asks. "Aren't we supposed to be happy? I get so confused when I see so many people walking around mad. What are they mad about? If something goes wrong, don't bitch. Go out and fix it! I don't have problems. I have challenges. We all have them. I just don't dwell on them. I find solutions."

Between countless athletic injuries, eighteen surgeries, and a lifestyle that made a twenty-four hour day at least fifteen minutes too short, Kramer's life, truly, has defied all medical and scientific odds.

"Even the boys in Vegas," he laughed.

Kramer played hard. He worked hard. He lived hard. Football injuries have left his body bent and battered. His less than conventional off-the-field adventures probably have added a few years to his true biological age.

But he wouldn't change a single day. He's still vibrant as a rookie racing into a game for his first play. Setbacks in life are only temporary inconveniences. Kramer prefers to use them as learning experiences.

"I've never had a bad day," he states with conviction. "How many people can say that? I've been on scholarship my whole life."

Despite not having played a game in more than forty years, Kramer's influence on college and professional football still is felt today.

"I call him 'The Legend,'" said Jim Brandstatter, former University of Michigan tackle and current radio broadcaster for both Michigan and the Detroit Lions.

"It's an overused term, but with him it's legitimate. When you look at everything he did in college and at the professional level, you have to pinch yourself to make sure you're not dreaming."

In a state that produced such sporting giants as Joe Louis, Charlie Gehringer, Magic Johnson, Dave DeBusschere, and Thomas Hearns, Kramer established himself as one of the purest athletes ever to emerge from Michigan.

Some say the best.

His pure athletic artistry and impact, however, are not restricted by geographic boundaries. Even more importantly, they transcend any particular period of history.

For true sports fans, fulfillment comes from debating the talents and accomplishments of players, teams, coaches, and managers as much as from watching the games themselves. Would Jim Brown have gained 20,000 career yards if he hadn't chosen to walk away from the game so early? Would Babe Ruth have hit a hundred home runs in a season given modern equipment and physical conditioning training? Would Bob Cousy be able to handle the quickness and power of Michael Jordan or LeBron James? In an old-fashioned head-butting contest, who would be the last man standing in a match between linebackers Dick Butkus and Ray Lewis?

There is no question that today's athletes are quicker, stronger, and in far better physical shape than those who preceded them. How many, though, from any era could shift from one sport to another without compromising at least a sliver of superiority from the sport that pays the bills? The purest of all athletes are those who gracefully slide from one sport to the next and still maintain an almost indescribable dominance for changing the course of a game, whatever it happens to be.

Comparison of athletes from different eras is best left to observers who are privileged to have witnessed the evolution of transition.

Jerry Green is a sports writer for the *Detroit News* and started with the Associated Press. He is semiretired from the *News* after spending more than a half-century covering all sports around the world. He is one of just a handful of writers to have covered every Super Bowl.

"Ron Kramer was absolutely dominant in every sport he played," Green remarked. "No matter the sport, he could change the course of a game single-handedly."

Ron Kramer celebrated his induction into the Michigan Sports Hall of Fame in 1971 with wife Nancy, daughter Cassie, and son Kurt.

As is Kramer, Green is a member of the State of Michigan Sports Hall of Fame. He remains renowned for his introspective point of view on all the games men play.

"I was privileged to cover a lot of great athletes," Green said after carefully considering a litany of celebrated performers. "I rate Gordie Howe and Bo Jackson as the top two pure athletes. Then it's Ron Kramer. He excelled in everything. He was an athlete in the true sense of the word. People that had a chance to see him perform were privileged. He was that dominating."

Diles agrees with his longtime Detroit colleague, with one significant amendment.

"I would put Kramer on a par with Jackson," Diles said. "Ron simply dominated any game he played. He was a big guy, but so graceful. There was a purity about the way Kramer attacked the game ... and also life. They don't make them like that anymore."

Boyd Dowler was one of the celebrated wide receivers and a teammate of Kramer on those storied Green Bay Packers teams. He echoes Green's sentiments.

"We had a lot of great athletes," Dowler reflected. "But Ron could do so much. He might have been our best pure athlete."

Bart Starr was the quarterback who reaped the benefits of having a tight end who could block a bull clear into the grandstands, then run a precise route to snag a pass over the middle on the very next play.

"We had all heard and read about what Ron had done at the University of Michigan," Starr said. "Then when you got to see his athleticism firsthand, it was overwhelming."

Dave Robinson enjoys a perspective from having played with and against Kramer. Robinson was an All Pro linebacker who joined the Packers in 1963. He then played against his former teammate when Kramer joined the Detroit Lions.

"I played against [Mike] Ditka, [Ray] Mackey, [Jackie] Smith, and [Charlie] Sanders," Robinson said. "They were all great, but none of them could carry Ron Kramer's jock strap. All of them could do one thing better than everyone else. Ron was the complete package—blocking, catching the ball, running. He also was a cerebral player. He never made any mental mistakes. He was the total package."

Joe Schmidt was a middle linebacker his whole career for the Detroit Lions and played his way into the NFL Hall of Fame. He was a teammate of Kramer late in Kramer's career before taking over as head coach of the Lions.

"Kramer was as good as any of those guys in the Hall of Fame ... or better," Schmidt said. "He did everything well—blocking, catching, and running good passing routes. He was blessed with a lot of talent. Above that was the passion he felt for the game. Every time he stepped on that field, you could feel it. That's what separates the great players from the average."

Gary Knafelc was an unheralded receiver who played for the Packers from 1954 through 1964. He never had the opportunity to see as many athletes as did Jerry Green. Knafelc was not a household name as were many of his teammates. He just happened to be the player from whom Kramer took the job. Although undersized for the position as Coach Lombardi envisioned it, he probably understood the role better than anyone except for Kramer himself.

"There's no doubt in my mind, he was the best pure athlete I have ever known," Knafelc said. "And I'm not just talking about football. He could have played linebacker. He could have played defensive end. He could have played any position on the field."

Knafelc, like the rest of the Packers, was well aware of Kramer's athletic exploits at the University of Michigan even before he arrived at his first training camp.

"I knew how good a basketball player he was," Knafelc said. "I played football and basketball for the University of Colorado and I wasn't able to touch him."

At the University of Michigan, Kramer set the standards by which nearly all athletic excellence is measured. Playing end on both offense and defense, he was a two-time consensus football All-American. His number 87 is one of only five numbers to have been retired by the winningest college football team in history. The others are 48, worn by former U.S. President Gerald R. Ford; 47, worn by Bennie Oosterbaan; 98, worn by Heisman Trophy winner Tom Harmon; and 11, worn by all three Wistert brothers (Francis, Albert, and Alvin).

Paul Hornung (*left*) and Ron Kramer combined to make the 1957 Green Bay draft, arguably, the best in NFL history.

Kramer was captain and led the basketball team in scoring and rebounds. In track he competed in the high jump, the shot put, and discus. He won nine varsity letters when freshmen were ineligible. He could have won more, but there just wasn't enough time in the day.

"I can't explain it," Kramer states with no false sense of humility. "Athletics always came easy. I could play anything ... even marbles."

Kramer was the first round draft choice of the Green Bay Packers in 1957. He also was drafted by the Detroit Pistons of the National Basketball Association.

"Think about that," said Paul Hornung. "Think about the history at the University of Michigan. I don't know of anyone doing all the things that Ron did."

Hornung won a Heisman Trophy playing for Notre Dame and then played his way into the NFL Hall of Fame running through the holes that Kramer helped to create for him.

Although a serious knee injury threatened to end his professional career shortly after it began, Kramer relentlessly rehabilitated himself only to make the rest of the National Football League pay the price.

Kramer was one of the architects of the tight end position as it is played today. And not for just any team. He did it for the Green Bay Packers of the early 1960s under legendary Hall of Fame Coach Vince Lombardi.

Kramer instilled new meaning into the emerging importance of the tight end. No longer was he just another lug at the end of the offensive line, designed to knock anyone wearing a different color jersey into the next morning. One play after leveling a defender with the thunder of a wrecking ball, he flashed the gentle touch of a pickpocket to grab a pass in the middle of traffic. Then he had the speed to move the ball down the field and the strength to drag a handful of defenders trying to wrestle him to the ground.

"I believe Ron could have played almost anywhere on the field," Starr said. "He was a tight end with the mind-set of a linebacker."

Lombardi marveled at the uncanny blend of brute and artist. Kramer's physical dominance allowed the coach to single block from the position. And wary defenders still had to guard against him slipping through a zone to take a pass all the way.

"It freed up another position," Lombardi once explained in reference to Kramer's intimidating blocking. "We didn't have to waste a player double-teaming a defender. It was like having a twelfth man on the field."

The Packers of the 1960s remain one of the most timeless teams in the history of professional sports. They set the standard for excellence by which teams still are measured today. Their trademark power sweep remains a signature as identifiable as the name Coke. They exhibited the discipline of a Swiss guard, providing an unstoppable force even to opponents aware of the coming play.

The mystique of those Packer teams actually transcended the games played on the field. During the infancy of network television football telecasts, they became "America's team" long before the Dallas Cowboys popularized the term.

"I remember my rookie year in 1957," Kramer recalled. "Bert Bell (NFL Commissioner) told us in a meeting that we were on the verge of something really big. He said that with television, the NFL was going to become the biggest thing to happen to television sports."

Those Packer teams laid the foundation for the billion dollar industry that exists today. They did it with more than might and mastery on the field. The players were a cast of colorful characters that spiked romance into the game.

Truly timeless teams are comprised of more than championships and gaudy statistics. Lombardi's Packers walked with an unmistakable swagger. The team was loaded with guys that jumped straight off the pages of a Damon Runyan novel. For six months of the year, they pounded each other mercilessly in practice, preparing to rip the arms and legs off their opponents each Sunday. For the other six months they worked at jobs just like their neighbors next door.

Off the field, some were living lyrics straight out of a Hank Williams Jr. get-down-and-rowdy country song. Yet on the field, they were as painfully precise as a hangman's new rope. Some never met a neon light that didn't look better when it was flashing just about midnight. But all were unforgiving when it came to what they expected of themselves once the cleats were laced up.

"We partied," Kramer admits. "Probably set some Olympic records. Once in a while, maybe even made the devil blush. But we never let it interfere with what had to be done on Sundays.

"We were good. Better than good. We were good because we had talent. We were disciplined and prepared for every situation.

There was a special kind of camaraderie. We were more of a family than just another football team."

Because they were hilariously human, memories of many make it seem as if they had played just last Sunday instead of almost a half-century ago. Names from that gloriously intimidating offense are as vivid as those playing today.

Bart Starr. Paul Hornung. Jim Taylor. Jim Ringo. Fuzzy Thurston. Jerry Kramer. Bob Skoronski. Forrest Gregg. Norm Masters. Boyd Dowler. Max McGee. Ron Kramer.

"How many teams were so good that everybody knew the names of the linemen?" Kramer asks.

The defensive side of the line featured just as many colorful luminaries.

"There's something about those Sixties teams that fans can't get enough of," said Green Bay Packers Hall of Fame archivist Tom Murphy. "They were so close to the fans. Stories get passed from one generation to the next."

Ron Kramer was more than just another player. Few, in fact, have left their fingerprints on college and professional football as indelibly as he. He is a member of the College Football Hall of Fame. Despite a laundry list of injuries that shortened his career, most former players believe he should be enshrined in the NFL Hall of Fame.

"Absolutely!" exclaimed Hornung. "Ron and Mike Ditka were the two best tight ends ever to play the game."

Players today are bigger. Some are stronger and perform at greater speed. It can be argued, nevertheless, that Kramer's innate athleticism would have allowed him to perform in any era.

"I wouldn't bet against him," Green said.

It begins with preparation and discipline. Kramer never forgets to remind himself each morning when he wakes up.

It's the only way to start a new day in the world according to Kramer.

2 *The House That Kramer Built*

For the last twenty years, Ron Kramer has done his early morning attitude adjustment in an anonymous speck on the Michigan map called Tyrone Township.

It's about an hour drive northwest of downtown Detroit, situated near such still semi-rural towns as Fenton and Holly. Even this once-remote area has succumbed slightly to urban sprawl. Still, there are enough open spaces, lakes, woods, and rolling hills to serve as a reminder that this was once a summer hideaway speckled with cottages owned by the wealthy of Detroit and the then-thriving automobile city of Flint.

Kramer's year-round hideaway is 120 acres, dense with oaks, pines, maples, firs, willows, and almost any other type of tree that Michigan has to offer. The serenity of the foliage is punctuated by a fifteen-acre, seventy-foot-deep, spring-fed lake. For years it was called Lake Kramer. It was renamed Samson after the death of his black Labrador. A wooden sign with a hand-painted picture of Samson is staked into the ground next to the dock.

"He was a great dog," Kramer said. "A regular member of the family. The special thing about dogs is that they're loyal."

Sitting atop a gentle hill in the middle of the postcard setting is a wood-framed, one-bedroom converted cottage as pretentious as a single log in a cord of wood stacked next to the barn. The undisturbed nature surrounding the modest home is a haven for a menagerie of wildlife that includes coyotes, foxes, beavers, deer, groundhogs, opossums, muskrats, skunks, squirrels, ducks, and a litany of species of birds long enough to make any ornithologist drool.

"I've got a zoo out here," Kramer proudly claims. "And they've got me. Who do you think got the better end of the deal?"

Kramer is kind to the healthy population of wildlife that he now considers part of his family. He merely leaves them all alone. And he observes.

"I learn so much watching all those critters," he says. "The beavers build dams all over the place. They're the greatest engineers on the face of the earth."

The contrast between the pastoral setting and the inside of Kramer's home is as stark as the forest's winter leafless branches compared to the lush richness of spring and summer's green. And it perfectly portrays the independent spirit that has driven Kramer's life since childhood.

"It's sort of a cross between the Smithsonian and the house they used to film the movie *Animal House*," he cracks.

Neither the Smithsonian nor *Animal House* may be quite so crammed with what Kramer simply refers to as "things."

"I've got a little bit of everything," he boasts with the pride of a pawnbroker who just happened to stumble his way into a diamond-studded Rolex. "I don't know where it all comes from. I just collect things."

The collection of "things" numbers 147,353—give or take a couple thousand. It consists of pictures, awards, letters, statues, gadgets, banners, pennants, footballs, helmets, jerseys, caps, sports memorabilia, rifles, shotguns, and a bazaar of knickknacks that would make any flea market manager turn thirteen different shades of green with envy.

The "things" cover the walls. They are crammed into corners and proudly circle the furniture like sentries. Even the paraphernalia is distinctly diverse.

Mounted to the wall near the ceiling of the indoor porch, for instance, is a twenty-five year limited-issue set of Hummel plates that Kramer started for his mother in 1971. Mounted on the kitchen back wall is a priceless set of 1928-issued plates depicting various scenes of the University of Michigan. The Wedgwood collection was made in England and purchased by Kramer at a flea market in nearby Linden, Michigan, a few years ago.

Both collections contrast sharply with a couple of Kramer's favorite doodads. A wooden duck sits defiantly just outside the kitchen and quacks wisecracks when unsuspecting visitors walk by. Some are innocently funny, like: "Tell me a joke and I'll quack up."

Or: "I love to eat quackers and jelly." Or: "Do you know when ducks get up in the morning ... at the quack of dawn."

Others are slightly risqué, like: "Want to see a new web site? Look between my legs."

Some of the eclectic material is preciously personal. The University of Michigan football jersey that Kramer wore in his last game is framed under glass and hangs above the fireplace. Kramer's number 87 was retired after his final game. Next to it is an "M Go Blue" bumper sticker that was taken to the moon. It was a gift to Kramer from former Michigan teammate Jack Lousma who served as a U.S. astronaut.

Hanging from the ceiling are such pertinent "things" as an elephant flying an airplane, a string of seashells, and wind chimes. One never knows, of course, when a strong breeze might whistle through the house. There are four bird feeders for any of Kramer's trapped aviary friends. There are four lacquered hornet nests taken from Kramer's endless stretch of woods.

"It amazes me how hornets and bees can construct such hives that withstand every element nature has to offer," Kramer said. "These four just didn't happen to survive Kramer. You can learn a lot from them."

A three-foot-tall stuffed doll of Oliver Hardy sits near the bay window in front of the outside deck. Stan Laurel used to sit next to him, but he was eaten by one of Kramer's dogs. A glass bust of W.C. Fields is appropriately placed near Oliver Hardy. There used to be a doll of Fields, but it became a gift to Paul Hornung, Kramer's longtime friend and former teammate.

"A true friend always knows what his buddy really wants," Kramer said.

An imposing figure in Kramer's collection is a three-foot lifelike replica of a rooster. He has strategically placed it atop a lampshade so it can vigilantly stare down a stuffed chicken in a nest that is suspended from the ceiling.

"That rooster is always prepared," he says. "Good attitude. I like that guy."

Framed photographs fight for each precious inch of wall space. A few are even attached to the ceiling. They portray a lifetime as eclectic as Kramer's collection of "things." The subjects range from such sports legends as Vince Lombardi, Paul Hornung, Mike Ditka, Jack Nicklaus, Bobby Knight, and Eddie Arcaro to one personally inscribed by former President Gerald Ford. Of course, several show

Kramer bulldozing his way through a wave of defenders when he played for Michigan, Green Bay, and the Detroit Lions.

Kramer's latest addition to his gallery of framed photos quickly became one of his favorites after he discovered it in his basement desk.

"Probably the greatest athlete I ever met," he says in reference to 1973 Triple Crown winner Secretariat. "It was like meeting Joe DiMaggio."

Kramer "met" the world's most famous horse since Mr. Ed while visiting the Claiborne Farm in Paris, Kentucky, in 1985. Claiborne is the celebrated breeding farm for the world's most famous racing thoroughbreds. It also is the burial ground for such luminaries as Swale and Riva Ridge.

Kramer was surprised when the keeper asked if he wanted the opportunity to touch the storied stallion.

"I watched the man walk into a barn and all of a sudden out walked Secretariat," he said. "He told me to touch him. It was like holding 150 million dollars in my hand."

The keeper, who was a rabid Packers fan, offered Kramer a special gift. He cut off a piece of Secretariat's mane and gave it to one of his favorite former players.

Kramer inserted part of the mane into the picture frame. He also framed three similar pictures, complete with a few strands of hair. Two went to former teammates Hornung and Mike Lucci. The other was given to longtime friend Glenn Wagner in honor of his fiftieth wedding anniversary.

"You don't get anniversary presents like that every year," Kramer said proudly.

The photos most precious, however, have nothing to do with sports. They are shots of Mom and Pop, Kramer's kids and grandkids, aunts, uncles, ex-wives, lady friends, and good buddies with whom Kramer has created so many memories.

"All good times and good people," Kramer says. "I can't remember who all is up there. I know there are some of my old girlfriends. Just because things didn't work out doesn't mean we can't be friends."

Kramer jokes with his lady friend, Barbara Giorgio, that his former girlfriends number "somewhere around a thousand."

"She calls herself number 1001," he cracked.

The basement and barn are as stuffed as the living area that Barbara kindly calls the "museum." Barbara and Kramer are good for each other. Even though the living space may be cluttered, Barbara knows that at least the bed will always be made.

"I have never been speechless in my life," Barbara said. "But the first time I saw the house I didn't say a word for fifteen minutes. He's got Beanie Babies stuffed into Lladro vases. Expensive wine glasses are scattered all over the place. I can tolerate it. I've learned to leave well enough alone."

The converted cottage is a sportsman's paradise and a woman's third-degree psychedelic nightmare.

"The things I collect are irreplaceable … if you know what I mean," he adds with a smile.

Kramer bought the house two days after he saw it in October 1987. The furniture he brought from his Bloomfield condo looked like props from a Star Trek feature film in his rustic refuge.

"Very early Jewish," he said. "Lots of mirrors and modern stuff. Nice, but they didn't have a place."

Perhaps nothing more precisely depicts the essence of Ron Kramer than this carefully created collection of mayhem that celebrates a lifetime of family, friends, fun, and … the discipline to have put it all together.

The character the house portrays was forged long before Kramer even knew he would settle into his personal slice of rustic Neverland.

Calling Kramer a character is like calling Groucho Marx a pretty funny guy. Kramer is hilariously human with a sense of honesty as blunt as a hammerhead. Don't ask him how he feels about something if you're not prepared to deal with the truth.

"Ron simply can't avoid the truth," said Dave Diles. "He's hard-nosed with a sense of humor. Not everyone understands his sensitivity and intelligence."

Kramer can be coarse. Many athletes who spend a career mauling opponents and getting blindsided themselves learn to shed the veneer in order to survive. He can be crude. A lifetime of locker rooms and too many good times with the boys are impossible to forget.

He's as mischievous as a shaggy-haired imp with an insatiable appetite for life that, at times, can be disconcerting to those who don't understand.

He's as subtle as a sledgehammer. Deep inside, however, he's as gentle as a speck of snow.

"He's like that big old dog that looks so mean everyone is afraid to pet him," said former Detroit teammate Joe Schmidt. "When you get to know him, though, you understand he's not that way at all. He's no phony. He doesn't try to hide who he is. What you see is what you get. He means no harm. It's his way of saying if you don't like what you see, just move on."

At Green Bay, former teammate and roommate Boyd Dowler didn't know how to take him at first.

"He prides himself on being a hard-ass," Dowler said. "But he's soft as a pillow inside."

Friends who knew Kramer long before he joined the Packers concur.

"He's mellowed, but there was a time when, in a crowd, he could be a real pain in the butt," said Dick Scott, a successful auto dealership owner who has known Kramer since high school. "One-on-one, he's the most caring and most gentle person you could ever meet. He's the best friend anyone could have."

Kurt Kramer agrees with the interpretations of those who know his father best.

"In the past, no doubt, people could be turned off by him," Kurt said. "I was. He was the original 'Good Time Charlie.'"

Peg Canham, widow of longtime University of Michigan Athletic Director Don Canham, remembers the first time she met Kramer thirty-two years ago. It was at a party the Canhams usually hosted the Friday evening before a Michigan football game. After the crowd departed, the Canhams, Kramer, and a handful of other former players went to a downtown Ann Arbor restaurant.

"They were the most obnoxious people I had ever been around," she recalled. "I never wanted to see this Kramer character again because he embarrassed everybody."

However, circumstances dictated that she did. At subsequent parties, Kramer would perform his infamous "eat a beer can trick."

"He would guzzle down a beer and then crush the can on his head," Canham recalled. "Then he would take a bite out of the can and chew on the piece."

Kramer smiled at the memory.

"But I never swallowed," he cracked.

Time allowed Peg to appreciate "this Kramer character" for who he really is.

"He was loud and gregarious," she said. "He loves having a good time and pushing the envelope a little bit. But he never intends to hurt anyone. People who act like that just for effect are phonies. Ron is not a phony. That's just Kramer. He doesn't apologize for who he is and that's what makes him so endearing. He's mellowed over the years. I consider him one of my best friends."

Kramer's mammoth size and sandpaper exterior belie the pussycat that lives inside.

"That's the Ron Kramer character that endears him to so many people," said former Michigan star Jim Brandstatter. "He can be coarse and crude. He is who he is and doesn't try to hide it. You have to look inside the package. That's where the real person lives.

"He's honest to a fault and more generous than Santa Claus. There are so many charities that he's supported over the years that nobody even knows about. And that's the way it stays because he won't allow it any other way. If someone needs ten bucks and that's all Ron has in his pocket, he coughs it up before that person has a chance to ask. Look past the rough edges and there's a man you're proud to call a friend."

Kramer doesn't just walk into a room. His presence explodes like an eight-point earthquake. He can be loquacious, even bombastic. But his gift for touch speaks louder than a litany of words. His handshake is convincing as a steel vice on a raw egg. He can "Kramer hug" a bear and loves to kiss a bald man on the top of his head. Sometimes even more.

"The first time I was kissed on the lips by a male was by Ron Kramer," Brandstatter laughed. "It was a joke, but that's just Kramer. The weird part about it, though, is now when I see him, I do it to him."

It's the Kramer character and how people expect that character to act.

Peg Canham witnessed Brandstatter's first male kiss.

"Ron is always kissing," she said. "He's very touchy. It's hard for a man to be that way and it says a lot about him. He doesn't care what people think. He's showing true affection. Obviously, he's not going to kiss someone he doesn't like. For a man to feel that comfortable inside his skin to be able to do that is special. Men who are not confident in themselves can't do it."

Brandstatter appreciates the Kramer character for his honesty.

"That's precisely why he's so colorful," Brandstatter is convinced. "He embraces the role similar to the way Jack Nicholson does his persona. Ron doesn't apologize for who he is. He's a genuinely caring person. If someone thinks he's a little off center, that's okay. It's perfectly normal to Ron. If people don't like it … see you next week."

Unfortunately for sports fans, such lovable human characters that spiked romance into the games are now more rare than dollar-a-gallon gasoline. Marketing madmen, the media, money—and corporate political correctness—have rendered them all but extinct.

"Some people ask why don't I change," Kramer said. "If I was going to change, I'd be a phony. No thanks. That's something I'll never be."

At 72, Kramer still looks forward to his next challenge. He's still the gritty street urchin who can't refuse any dare. And he's suspicious of those who refuse to give or accept them.

"What the hell good is life if you can't accept a challenge?" he asks. "Let's not take things so seriously. Life's supposed to be fun. Let's have a few laughs."

That's the Ron Kramer character—disciplined enough to make it work.

3 *Discipline ... Discipline ... Discipline*

Ron Kramer's introduction to discipline came at the end of a four-foot leather strap that his father used to sharpen his straight razor. Kramer still keeps the strap in the basement office of his home and smiles appreciatively every time he sees it.

"My mother and father taught me the value of discipline at a very early age," he recalls. "When I didn't catch on quick enough, Pop went to the strap. He never beat me. He used it just enough to get the message across."

Kramer once took the strap with him to make a point at a D.A.R.E. presentation at a local school.

"Kids need to be disciplined," he says. "If they don't get it from their parents, who are they going to get it from? That's the problem today. Nobody wants to be disciplined."

No day passes without Kramer silently thanking his parents for the lessons they imparted. Preparation and discipline were stressed as much as brushing his teeth before going to bed. They taught him that discipline is the bridge to proper preparation. And preparation is the most direct line to successful performance.

"I was performing since day one," Kramer said. "And I was always prepared."

He had to be. His mother's sister married one of his father's brothers. And his mother's brother married his father's sister.

"It was like having three sets of parents," Kramer chuckled. "That's a recipe for a lot of discipline. The pickings for partners must have been slim in ol' Fifty Camp."

Fifty Camp was a small coal mining town near Pittsburg, Kansas. It sat, not so coincidentally, adjacent to Fifty-One Camp.

Kramer's father, John, came from Fifty-One. His mother, Adeline, came from Fifty.

John's formal education ended after the third grade when he could walk to school without the bottom side of his lunch bucket scraping the ground. That was induction time for the mines in Fifty-One Camp. All families shared crops from their farms in the tiny villages.

First the devastating dust storms and later the Great Depression sent families from all the camps scurrying to survive. Men wandered from town to town looking for any kind of work to support their wives and children. Some took to the highway and used their thumbs to beg a ride from a kindly passing driver. Others hopped trains and wound up in cities far from the heartland.

"They were hoboes," Kramer said. "They had to be. They did anything they could to support their families."

John found his way to Detroit where the automotive industry was booming. He landed a job in the Chevrolet Forge Plant in Hamtramck, a small bustling city enclosed on all four sides by Detroit.

Those were the days when steel for axles and other automobile parts was forged by hand. It was dangerous, dirty, hard, gritty work. After thirty-eight years, John retired from the same plant and never missed one day of work.

In 1967, Kramer experienced one of the most gratifying experiences of his life. It occurred in the office of General Motors Corporation President Ed Cole. Kramer was a cofounder of the Walter Hagen Golf Classic to benefit the American Cancer Society. He had secured Cole to serve as honorary chairman.

"I used to know a Kramer that worked at Chevrolet Forge," Cole said.

"That was my father," Kramer replied.

Cole rose from his chair and walked slowly toward the retired football legend.

"Let me tell you something, son," Cole began. "When I graduated from General Motors Institute, they put us all through hell. And that forge plant was nothing but pure hell. I worked for your father for two months and learned more in those two months than at any time during my career. He was the best forge man I ever met."

Kramer was stunned. For the first time in his life he was, perhaps, a little tongue-tied.

Life on the farm was tough for Grandpa John Kramer, who stands next to Ron's mother Adeline.

Grandma Anna Marie Tschiltsch shows Ron the fine art of rocking on a swing once he returned from hunting.

The fish were biting for (*left to right*) Uncle Paul, cousin Ken, Harry, Ron, Papa John, and Anna Marie.

Aunt Margaret Kramer looks at Anna Marie and Ron as Grandpa Godfrey and Grandma Anna Marie Tschiltsch stand proudly by a stack of hay on the Kansas farm.

John and Adeline Kramer stand proudly with Ron, while mom holds
sister Anna Marie, at their home in Detroit.

Ron Kramer owes his sense of discipline to his father, John, who obviously enjoyed a sense of humor, too.

"Can you imagine how proud I felt?" he said. "Here I was an All-American football player. I played for the champion Green Bay Packers. I played in a Pro Bowl. And then to hear the president of General Motors say that about my father ... it topped any honor that I had ever received."

Just prior to Kramer's birth in 1935, his mother returned to Kansas for the delivery of her son.

"She didn't trust the doctors up here," he explained. "She went back home and I was born midwifed by my grandmother."

While Kramer's father sweat in the factory, his mother worked in the cafeteria at East Detroit High School. Needless to say, her attendance record was also unblemished.

"I had to go to school every day," Kramer cracked. "I had no choice. My father never missed a day of work. Neither did my mother. She was working right in the school and knew where everybody was all the time. My senior year I tried to skip one day and got caught in the first ten minutes."

It was in East Detroit (now called Eastpointe) where Kramer learned to play all his games. In the streets or in the parks, it didn't matter to Kramer and his gang, who have remained friends for life. Football in the fall. Basketball in the winter. Baseball in the spring and summer. They even managed to squeeze in a little bit of street hockey if a basketball court wasn't open.

"Ron beat everybody in everything he tried," recalled Ron Klug who has remained friends with him since the second grade. "We had a pool table in the basement. After playing one time, he could whip anyone. He always had so much confidence that he would win. It was a joy just to watch him compete."

Some of Kramer's athletic feats remain playground legend.

"He was the first guy I ever saw stand flat-footed under a basket and jump high enough to stuff it into the net," Dick Scott said. "Think about that. Nobody dunked a ball back then."

Nothing was more important than family to the Kramers, who were first-generation Americans from Austria. Each summer when Kramer and his sister, Anna Marie, were finished with school, Adeline would return to Kansas so that her kids would get to know their grandparents. Before school resumed in the fall, John would take his two-week vacation to pick up his family for the return to Detroit.

During those summers, Kramer worked the farms where the older generation refused to leave.

Kramer was a pudgy little center on the football team in junior high. When he returned from Kansas for his freshman year of high school, he had shed his baby fat and grown six-and-a-half inches. The coach, who had known him all his life, didn't recognize him. He asked Kramer what school he had transferred from.

It didn't take long for Kramer to launch an athletic career still unmatched in Michigan high school history.

As a freshman he was called up to the varsity for the last games of the season in football and basketball. As a sophomore, no one could stand in his way. In his sophomore year, East Detroit won its football league championship. After a collection of talented seniors graduated, the next two years were lean. They were known as the seasons of "Kramer and the ten dwarfs."

At some point, Kramer played almost every position on both sides of the line. When the offense needed a few yards for a first down, Kramer moved to fullback. If a pass was needed, he was the target. If a hole needed to be opened on the line, the ball carrier followed Kramer.

Kramer also moved around on defense to confuse opponents who often triple-teamed him. He could run. He could catch. He could kick. He could punt. And he could knock an opponent into the next county without even realizing the force with which he hit.

The legend still lives about the game in which he amassed more than thirty tackles.

"I never counted," Kramer said. "I just wanted to win and knock some people silly."

Kramer isn't certain why the games came so naturally to him.

"I never gave it much thought," he said. "I guess I was just born with talent. But I always disciplined myself to be prepared to make the most of it."

Before his senior season ended, every major college came courting with a four-year scholarship in hand. Michigan, Michigan State, Notre Dame, Ohio State, Oklahoma, and the Naval Academy were just a handful. He had his pick of schools for both football and basketball.

There was never any doubt in Kramer's mind about which school he was going to choose. He didn't want to waste anyone's time. He selected the University of Michigan so that his parents could watch him play.

"Make a decision and move on," he said. "I've been that way all my life."

John and Adeline's devotion to their son's full plate of athletic activities was fiercely loyal and perhaps unmatched. When Kramer competed in football, basketball, and track for East Detroit High School, his parents attended each game and meet. When Kramer moved up to the University of Michigan, they drove to each home and away football game. So, too, did Kramer's younger sister, Anna Marie, and his friend Ron Klug.

"At the time, I didn't know all the things Ron had accomplished," Anna Marie recalled. "I always cheered for him because he was my brother. It wasn't until years later I realized how good he really was. I am so proud of him."

Kramer savored his family support. It was the only thing he knew.

"The only Michigan game they missed was my first one," Kramer said. "That was the one against Washington in Seattle."

Their devotion to Michigan football didn't end with Kramer's graduation in 1957. John and Adeline attended all home games until John died in 1972. That didn't stop Adeline. She continued to attend all home games until her death in 1988. From 1953 through 1987, she attended 241 consecutive home games, always in seats 24 and 25 in row 83 of section 2.

"Everybody knew her," Kramer proudly says. "Rain, snow, sleet, it didn't matter. Neither did the score. She never left that game till it was over."

Kramer recalls one miserably wet afternoon when he took his mom to the game in a camper with a group of his friends. Mom wanted to sit in her usual seats. Kramer and his friends watched the game from the other side of the field. Once Michigan put the game out of hand, Kramer's boys were itching to leave to get dry and beat the crowd.

"Wait a minute," Kramer said. "You're forgetting someone."

The party couldn't leave until Mom, ten pounds heavier from her soaking clothes, greeted the players as they departed the locker room.

"That was Mom," Kramer said. "She was beautiful."

Ironically, she sat in row 83—the number Kramer wore for the Detroit Lions; she saw her last game in '87—the number he wore for Michigan; and she died in '88—the number he wore for the Green Bay Packers.

Kramer's son, Kurt, now holds the Michigan tickets.

At a school like the University·of Michigan where tradition is valued as much as another victory, the Kramer family established one that may never be replaced.

4 *Is It Really Me?*

The summer before Ron Kramer's senior year in high school, his father took him to the Chevrolet Forge Plant for an up-close look at factory life.

Inside the plant, the temperature was blistering hot. Hammers pounded. Sparks flew. Sweat poured from the men as they turned steel into workable forms to fit axles and various designs of the shiny new cars. The pounding, clanging, and grunting became a synchronized cacophony to which workers' ears had become immune. Even in the dead of winter, the heat from the giant furnaces mixed with the sweat from the weary workmen to produce a ubiquitous moisture that simply hung in the air all year long.

"If that had been today, the plant would be shut down," Kramer said. "They must have broken every safety rule and regulation. When I was thirteen I put 2,000 bales of hay up on the farm in Kansas in 115 degree heat. That was nothing compared to what went on in the plant."

John Kramer's silent lesson was subtle but successful. His son could follow his footsteps to a reliably tedious future in the factory. Or he could take a brave new step that no other member of the Kramer family had ever attempted.

"It didn't take long to decide," Kramer said. "Ten days and I was out. Pop made his point. I spent the rest of the summer working on a garbage truck to pick up a few bucks before going back to school."

The factory visit convinced Kramer about what he wanted to do. It also affirmed his appreciation for his father who never missed a day of work in thirty-eight years at the plant.

"That's discipline," Kramer said. "And I got the chance to go to school with all expenses paid."

Football and basketball served as Kramer's ticket to a degree from one of the leading academic universities in the country. The University of Michigan was a perfect fit for Kramer. He could get an education and his family could watch him play all the games that had become part of the Kramer family life. His early years of discipline already provided rewards.

Though much of the Ann Arbor campus remains the same, the university in 1953 had a totally different personality than it does today. It was the Eisenhower years and America was at peace. Television was in its infancy and people were just getting used to having Ed Sullivan visit their living rooms on Sunday evenings. Lucille Ball and Desi Arnaz would drop by on Mondays. Milton Berle was a welcomed guest on Tuesdays.

Drive-in restaurants were popping up in large cities. Perry Como was the hottest singer on TV. And the world had yet to be shaken with the coming of Elvis. Students fashioned penny loafers with khaki pants and collared shirts. Letter sweaters were the norm for athletes privileged to represent their schools. Coeds wore plaid skirts and an appropriate measure of morning make-up. Friday mixers in the Student Union provided opportunity for opposite sexes to meet.

They weren't necessarily better times. They were simply different.

"The Fifties were great years," Kramer recalled. "They were learning years. We partied. We drank. But there were no drugs or anything like that. The biggest thing we ever did was have a panty raid one time."

Significantly different was the absence of protests.

"We went to school to learn," Kramer said. "When I went to school it wasn't as crazy as it is now. There's a place to be liberal and a place to have discipline. Our educational system has to teach discipline. You don't just do your own thing when you leave school. This is still a team. It's called America. If you have everyone going off on tangents, you lose track of what we're here for."

Kramer had a first-hand encounter with protest when his son, Kurt, was in grade school. A teacher had Kurt's class make signs to protest pollution for a demonstration outside of the school. Kramer asked his son what they did with the signs after the protest.

"We threw them in the trash can," Kurt answered.

"And what do they do with the trash?" Kramer asked.

Kurt looked confused.

"They burn it," Kramer said emphatically. "And that puts smoke into the air!"

Kramer jumped into his car and immediately drove to the school.

"If you ever do this to my son again, you ain't going to be teaching here very long because I'm going to bust you," he informed the teacher in less than diplomatic terms.

In the 1950s, however, protests were nothing more than parts of court cases and union negotiations. They had no place on any college campus.

"When I went to Michigan, I wanted to make my whole family proud," Kramer said. "When I played for Michigan and Green Bay and Detroit, I was doing it for my whole family. I wanted them to say: 'That's our Ronnie.'"

Kramer entered the University of Michigan without any apprehension about the sports in which he would compete. He was better than anyone and knew it. He had prepared well and only needed the opportunity to shine.

This is Kramer's favorite handoff—to son Kurt. All the honors were great, but nothing is as precious to Kramer as family.

The aura of Michigan, however, was something totally foreign. While he had been a good high school student, he felt unprepared for university life.

No Kramer had ever gone to college. He had to rely on instinct and learn from his new friends. Tom Maentz was the "other" end of Michigan's dynamic duo. Kramer played left end and Maentz was on the right.

"Tom and I became great friends," Kramer said. "His father had graduated from Michigan and owned a bank in Holland [Michigan]. His mother went to college. I watched Tom and Terry Barr and some of the other guys. Tom and Terry always seemed to know what to do. It was all new to me."

For Michigan, Barr was an outstanding halfback who reunited with Kramer as teammates after Kramer was traded to the Detroit Lions.

"I'm still flattered that Ron looked up to me for something," Barr smiled. "It seems like it was always the other way around. I have been fortunate to know many great athletes. None were as gifted as Ronald J. Kramer. He was special. He could do everything. If I was in a fight, I'd want him on my side.

"He might be a little different. Underneath, though, he truly cares about people. I am blessed to have been his friend and teammate."

Retired, renowned multimedia journalist Dave Diles appreciates Kramer's early apprehensions of going to the University of Michigan. Diles is an Ohio native and grew up under the overwhelming influence of Ohio State.

"I had heard all the stories about Michigan," Diles recalled. "When I got there, though, I discovered that Michigan stood for everything good. I met a different class of person and different class of athlete.

"Ron Kramer became the quintessential Michigan Man. He had a swagger and took his job seriously, but never himself. Shakespeare wrote 'the play is the thing.' Well, Kramer could play and let it do all the talking."

To conquer any apprehensions he harbored about college life, Kramer practiced what he'd taught himself to do in high school. He studied his environment and learned the best way to survive. He showed up each day on time for all his classes. He completed all assignments in a timely fashion. He made a point of getting to know his instructors.

In his senior year, Kramer struggled with a mandatory Spanish class he needed to pass in order to graduate.

"I had to get to know that teacher very well," Kramer said. "I only got a 'C' for the course, but I made it to graduate."

Kramer had been a one-man highlight film for three years on the football field in the Big House. Yet no single day meant as much to him as commencement day, held on the same field on which he had starred.

"I was fortunate to win a lot of athletic awards," he said. "The thing I'm proudest of at Michigan, though, is that I got my degree in four years."

Kramer earned a B.S. with a major in psychology. He took fifteen hours each semester with no special schedule consideration because of his hectic athletic responsibilities.

"It's not like what they do now," Maentz recalled. "We stood in line with all of the other students to register for classes. We had to fit them in the best we could. Ron and I had an astronomy course at 9 a.m. and had to hustle to be on time for the team bus for road trips on Fridays."

Despite juggling his time between football and basketball games and practices, along with track meets, Kramer—like his father at work—never missed a class.

Kramer's acclimation to university life was enhanced by his membership in Sigma Chi Fraternity. It was the security of family that provided a feeling of belonging. Following his professional career, Kramer received a distinguished alum award from the fraternity.

"I don't know how he did it with all of his time constraints, but he became real active," Maentz said. "Every year we hosted a mother's weekend at the frat house. Ron's mom was a little like him. Kind of feisty, but very nice. She would dance all night. She taught Ron how to do the Charleston, the Jitterbug, the Black Bottom, and all the dances."

A few years later with the Green Bay Packers, Kramer's dancing skills were put to good use. The Packers were playing the Rams in Los Angeles and were staying in a hotel on Muscle Beach. Kramer was rooming with wide receiver Max McGee who picked up a girl that wanted to go dancing.

"Krames," McGee pleaded. "I've got a date with this beautiful girl, but she wants to go dancing and do the Cha-Cha-Cha."

What's a roommate for if he can't teach his buddy how to Cha-Cha-Cha?

"We were both in our skivvies going 'one, two—Cha-Cha-Cha,'" Kramer said. "Suddenly the door opened and the maid walked in. Her mouth dropped to the floor. She said she'd come back later. We laughed our asses off. Those were the days when it wasn't popular to even look like you're gay."

Psychology, sports, and dancing. The university life certainly provided a well-rounded education for Kramer.

5 *The Legend Begins*

The legend of Kramer grew quickly at Michigan. Though fresh out of high school, his athletic superiority was impossible to ignore. Had he played in modern times, he would have started in the Big House on his first Saturday in Ann Arbor.

Few questioned how dominant he was to become.

College football, however, was still decades away from its billion-dollar-a-year television spectacle. Administrators stood relentlessly firm that freshmen needed a year to acquaint themselves with the rigors of academic life. That noble ideal stood proudly for decades.

Isn't it peculiar how quickly even the most noble ideal is compromised in the face of money too large for university presidents and administrations to ignore?

There was a freshman team for players like Kramer and Tom Maentz and Terry Barr. All wound up playing in the National Football League. They practiced all week and spent Saturday afternoons watching the varsity from the stands.

Even in practice, however, the buzz about Kramer grew louder as the season crept along.

"The things he could do were uncanny," Maentz marveled. "He was a fierce, deadly blocker. He made impossible catches look easy. He was an inspiration to all of us. He elevated our own abilities. In my mind, he was the best all-around athlete of our era."

The football field was only one of Kramer's domains. He loved basketball as much as any other sport. Often after freshman practice, he sneaked into Yost Field House, slipped on a pair of gym shoes, and dared anyone to take him on in a game of one-on-one.

In 1956, Ron Kramer captained the University of Michigan basketball team and led the team in scoring and rebounding.

The previous winter, Maentz had been a standout on the Holland (Michigan) High School team that advanced late into the state tournament.

"I took him on," Maentz said with a smile. "He didn't have any trouble picking my pocket. I knew then and there what kind of special athlete he was."

Kramer also smiles at the memory.

"Tom came from a fine family," Kramer said. "They had a tennis court and basketball court in their backyard. He just never had the opportunity to play on the street like we did."

Kramer continued to amaze his teammates and Sigma Chi brothers. Once, in the frat house, he was found in the basement playing ping-pong for the first time.

"He was playing a Chinese kid who was awfully good," Maentz said. "Ron beat him without even breaking a sweat. It really didn't matter what game Ron played. He always found a way to beat you."

Perhaps the most humorously amazing physical feat Maentz had ever witnessed, however, occurred at a party a few years after graduation. It happened during the winter when the Twist was the new dance craze.

"There was an ice-skating rink and everyone was skating," Maentz said. "All of a sudden there was Ron doing the Twist on skates while balancing a martini on his head. And he never spilled a drop."

Throughout his career with Green Bay and long afterward, the "martini on the head dance" became one of Kramer's standards.

"He's got two new knees, two artificial hips, and he can still do it without spilling a drop," said longtime friend Dick Scott. "It still amazes me."

Kramer merely laughs at the dexterity of his head.

"I honestly don't know how that started," he smiled. "I guess I was at some party and somebody dared me to try it. All it required

Ron Kramer on the field in a 1954 University of Michigan game against Iowa. (Reproduced by permission from Bentley Historical Library, University of Michigan)

was moving your body without moving your head. I guess I was pretty good. A lot of people remember. And it's a good way to get a free martini."

Football, of course, was to become Kramer's identity. The lifestyle it was to provide had been unimaginable during his four years in Ann Arbor.

Coach Bennie Oosterbaan was eager for his prodigy to be eligible for the varsity in the fall of 1954. He knew the talent that was just waiting to explode. Oosterbaan planned to unleash it any way he could.

Oosterbaan used Kramer at tight end, defensive end, running back, quarterback, and receiver. At times, all in one game. Kramer also kicked extra points and field goals. It was at tight end where he truly excelled. His blocking and tackling skills were among the best in the nation.

Michigan ran a winged-tee offense, so passing in those days was minimal. When the opportunity to catch a pass arose, however, Kramer rarely missed an opportunity to tuck the ball under his arm and drag a couple of overmatched defenders a few more yards down the field. And it usually came at one of the most critical points of the game.49

Oosterbaan paid him the highest compliment when he said: "To top off his marvelous physical gifts of size and speed and strength, plus an uncanny coordination, Kramer was one of the fiercest competitors I've ever seen. Nothing was impossible for him—the impossible was only a challenge."

Oosterbaan marveled at Kramer's uncompromising commitment to whatever sport he happened to be playing. The coach sometimes had to harness his protégé in the face of serious injury.

In the 1955 game against Army, Terry Barr was returning a kickoff with Kramer running downfield interference. Kramer took a helmet to the chest from one of the Cadets, resulting in a collapsed lung and seven broken ribs. He was hospitalized until the following Friday. On Saturday, he ordered the trainer to tape him tightly in order to play the game against Northwestern.

Oosterbaan appreciated Kramer's determination, but refused to let his meal ticket play. His compromise was to allow him to dress and sit on the bench for the game. The coach also allowed Kramer to travel to Minnesota the following Saturday, but again kept him from taking the field.

Finally, Iowa was scheduled to visit Ann Arbor and the game was too critical for Kramer to miss. Taped like a mummy, he finally returned and threw a bone-crunching block on a helpless Hawkeye to spring Maentz loose for a touchdown that triggered a come-from-behind 34–21 victory.

"Pain is part of the game," Kramer explains. "You can't cry about it. If you can't take it, don't go on the field."

Howard "Hop-a-Long" Cassady won the Heisman Trophy playing for Ohio State University in 1955. He learned to appreciate Kramer's work ethic in history's most celebrated college football rivalry.

"You had to know where he was every minute of the game," Cassady recalled. "His presence had to be accounted for. He had the greatest ability. He was big, strong, and fast. Man, he hit hard.

A "really big show" is what TV legend Ed Sullivan called his telecast of the All-America team that included Kramer of Michigan wearing his number 87 that was retired after his senior season and John Witte of Oregon State. (Reproduced by permission from Bentley Historical Library, University of Michigan)

He was a clean player, though. He never took any cheap shots. He didn't need to. I don't think he ever got called for a fifteen-yard penalty. He was good enough to hit anybody straight on."

The two became friends and actually worked together for Paragon Steel once their playing careers ended.

"Ron is a tremendous person," Cassady said. "He was big, tough and loved to have fun … still does."

Kramer didn't win the Heisman. Even at the less glamorous position of end, however, he was elected to the College Football Hall of Fame.

He was a consensus All-American in his junior and senior seasons. Unlike today, that was a time of only one generally accepted All-American team. Only twelve players were honored, and they were feasted in the fashion of the prestigious award.

All were flown to New York for appearances on the *Ed Sullivan* and *Perry Como* TV shows. On the *Sullivan* show, Kramer got to meet Pearl Bailey, one of his favorite singers. After the *Como* show, all twelve players were hosted to dinner at the Copacabana by entertainer Jimmy Durante.

The ceremonies also initiated a lifelong friendship between Kramer and one of his soon-to-be Green Bay teammates. Hall of Famer Paul Hornung was also named to the All-American team.

"Kathy Crosby was a guest on the Sullivan show," Kramer recalled with a smile. "Hornung tried to take a shot at her. She said she'd go to dinner with him, but she was traveling with an entourage of fourteen and Paul passed. He also took a shot at Kim Novak. He was a beauty … still is."

Kramer was impressed by the hoopla, but remained grounded enough to realize he didn't win the honor by himself.

"I accepted the honor on behalf of everybody," he explained. "For my teammates, my coaches, and for my school. No one is good enough to be All-American by himself."

At the annual football banquet following his senior season in 1956, Kramer's number 87 was retired by Coach Oosterbaan. Only five numbers in the 127 years of Michigan football history have been so honored.

Over the years, Kramer has had time to truly appreciate the meaning of that distinction.

"At the time it happened, I had no idea what it meant," he said. "I was busy getting ready for the basketball season. It took me a while to realize it's now part of the Michigan tradition."

Occasionally, Kramer drops in to Michigan practices during the season. Former player Jim Brandstatter remembers the first time he saw the man he calls "The Legend."

"Michigan is built on tradition," Brandstatter said. "Fielding H. Yost. Fritz Crisler. Bo Schembechler. Tom Harmon. All these legends. So when Ron Kramer came around, it definitely got your attention. He's part of the building blocks upon which all that tradition is built.

"His number is retired. He played for Bennie Oosterbaan. Kramer and Tom Maentz were on the cover of *Sports Illustrated*. When you're a kid, all this stuff has been processed by your brain and you're following in that tradition. When Ron Kramer shows up, he's not Ron Kramer. He's this bigger-than-life history book character. I was in awe."

So were a lot of other people at the tradition Kramer created.

6   *"My Name Is Kramer"*

Some first impressions fade with time. Those of Ron Kramer remain like an indelible tattoo.

Sam Huff was a rugged New York Giants middle linebacker who scrapped his way into the National Football League Hall of Fame. The Giants were the defending NFL champions when they played the College All-Stars in the 1957 preseason exhibition opener at Chicago's Soldier Field.

Huff still smiles at his first Kramer encounter.

"I had heard and read about all the things he had done at the University of Michigan, so he wasn't exactly an unknown," Huff recalled. "Our first encounter on the field, though, was a little bit out of the ordinary."

Kramer caught a pass and was moving up the field. Huff grabbed him from behind and had trouble bringing him down.

"He was a big son of a gun and ran good for his size," Huff said. "I tried to strip the ball from his arms."

That's when Kramer made his unforgettable impression.

"As I was trying to take the ball away, he tried to push me off and punched me," Huff said. "Can you imagine that? Here's a kid who hadn't played one pro game. We were the defending champions, and he hauls off and punches me."

After Huff hog-tied him to the ground, he returned a smack to Kramer's head that caught the attention of a referee.

"He flagged me for a fifteen-yard penalty," Huff said. "It was third down and that gave them a first. That's a basic no-no."

When the Giants huddled for the next play, linebacker Bill Swoboda was livid.

"Who the hell got that penalty?" he screamed.

Swoboda was the captain and tough enough to gargle broken

glass. When Huff admitted to the infraction, more fireworks exploded.

"I told him it was me," Huff said. "Then he hauled off and smacked me and told me to get off the field for a play. I got hit by both sides. That was my introduction to Ron Kramer."

Another standout NFL linebacker treasures a pair of unforgettable Kramer encounters.

Mike Lucci was playing for the Cleveland Browns when he first met Kramer, before the two became teammates on the Detroit Lions.

Cleveland and Green Bay were meeting in what was generally termed the "Runner-up Bowl" in 1964. It was a time when the second-place finishers of each division played against each other with the players picking up a few extra dollars before the official start of the off-season. The game was in Miami and Lucci used the occasion to celebrate his honeymoon with his wife, Pat.

The newlyweds were sharing cocktails in the Dream Bar when they noticed a hulking figure spinning around the dance floor with a martini on his head. Lucci was fascinated. Not a drop was being spilled.

"I think I know that guy," Lucci told his wife. "That's Ron Kramer. I'm going to play against him in the game."

Shortly after Nancy and Ron graduated from the University of Michigan in 1957, the pair made a spectacular wedding couple.

When the music stopped, Kramer quickly drank his martini and triumphantly returned to the table with wife Nancy. The couple were with a gang of Packers who never ran into a party they didn't appreciate.

Lucci approached Kramer's table to introduce himself. After all, the two were going to bang heads with each other in a few days. Even more importantly, Lucci had to find out how Kramer could dance with a full martini glass on his head without spilling a drop.

"Because I don't like to waste a perfectly good martini," Kramer explained simply.

The two couples spent the rest of the evening together celebrating the upcoming game, the end of the season, and the newlyweds. As the evening moved past midnight, the two ladies decided to call it a night.

The couples returned to their rooms, but not before Kramer and Lucci secretly agreed to return for a few final rounds after the wives had fallen asleep.

"We got plastered," Kramer smiled. "I tried to teach Lucci how to dance with the glass on his head. I guess you have to be born with that kind of talent."

Slightly before daybreak, the two opposing buddies tiptoed into their rooms. Kramer fell asleep on the floor. Lucci's return was not quite so subtle.

"Pat was furious," Kramer recalled. "She started to pack her clothes to go home."

Calmness obviously prevailed. The Luccis have been married for more than forty years, just slightly longer than Kramer and Lucci have been best friends.

Not quite so dramatic, but equally memorable, was the first time Lucci set eyes on Kramer.

"Mike Ditka and I were freshmen at the University of Pittsburgh," Lucci said. "Michigan came to town for a basketball game, and we were watching the varsity play. We looked at each other and said, 'Who is that big son of a bitch out there for Michigan?' Pitt had a big center and Kramer was beating the living hell out of him. In the second half, Kramer had him shooting from the outside. There was no way he was going to slug it out with Kramer under the basket anymore."

Ironically, Kramer, Lucci, and Ditka all went on to star in the National Football League. Ditka played his way into the National Football League Hall of Fame and then coached the Chicago Bears to a Super Bowl championship. Lucci was with the Lions when Kramer went to Detroit. The two became roommates and have remained best friends.

The night before the last game of the 1965 season, the Lions' players threw a party to celebrate. Lucci decided to remain in the room and took a sleeping pill before going to bed.

"I woke up about three or four in the morning and saw that Kramer's bed was empty," Lucci laughed. "A little later, I heard some banging on the door. I opened it, and there's Ron, lying in the hall against the door.

"At 6:30, he's in the shower singing and having a grand old time. He went out and made three or four catches and had a helluva game. I didn't get any sleep and scuffled all day. He was amazing."

Lucci still marvels at the way Kramer was always prepared

Ron Kramer may have gone down after making a shot for the University of Michigan, but someone was going to pay a price.

for any situation. While playing for Cleveland against Green Bay, Lucci still can't believe one play that he saw.

"He caught a pass against us and was close to going out of bounds," Lucci said. "He flipped the ball over his head to Boyd Dowler who took it down the field."

Had ESPN been in existence at the time, the play would have remained a highlight for weeks.

"I was trailing on the play," Dowler recalled. "Ron had a hand around the defender's throat, pushing him down the field. It looked like he was strangling him. I was yelling at him to flip me the ball. He looked around and said: 'Just a minute, you son of a bitch, I'll get it to you. Can't you see I'm kind of busy now?'"

Even before watching Kramer dance with the martini on his head, Lucci was convinced of Kramer's athletic abilities when he witnessed that basketball game in Pittsburgh several years before.

Kramer had his own style of playing basketball. For a man his size, he had a surprisingly soft shot. He could even handle the ball a little. Despite being undersized, he could dunk a basketball from the time he was a junior in high school.

The heart of his game, however, was to protect the real estate beneath the basket. Those who dared to trespass did so at their own risk. It would have made a good script for an episode of professional wrestling.

"The contact wasn't bad," Kramer deadpanned. "It was for the opposing players, but not for me. I was used to getting really whacked around on the football field. If I was guarding a seven-footer, I'd keep him out at the foul line and he couldn't get a rebound. Besides, what good is a game without a little contact? It's good for the soul."

Lucci and Ditka became quickly convinced about Kramer's dominance.

"That game I watched him play, he absolutely punished our center," Lucci said.

Kramer started at center for three years at Michigan and was captain of the team as a senior. By the time he left school, he was the school's all-time scoring champion with 1,124 points. No one knows how many rebounds he grabbed. Statistics weren't as sophisticated then as they are now. Anyone who saw him play, however, knows he gobbled up rebounds like a ten-year-old raiding a jar full of cookies. It was impossible to get in his way without paying the price.

Although he was Green Bay's first round draft choice, the

Detroit Pistons also picked him in the National Basketball Association draft. Practicing with the Pistons, Kramer performed as what he called a "fire chief."

"If somebody was hot, they sent me in to put him out," he said. "They put me on the floor and told me to play guard. I was going against Gene Shue. I roughed him up so bad, the coach called time and told me to move to forward. Shue was his boy and the heart of the team. They couldn't afford to let him get hurt."

Although he didn't last with the Pistons, during one football off-season, he played for a Grand Rapids, Michigan, semipro team and received one hundred dollars a game.

"The first game I played, we beat a hotshot team from Gary, Indiana," Kramer said. "I hit a shot at the buzzer to win the game. We all went out and partied and there went the hundred bucks. Then I had to drive back to Detroit in a blizzard. But it was fun and it kept me in shape for football."

Bob Vander Werf, a former captain of the Central Michigan University basketball team, played on that semipro club and became lifelong friends with Kramer.

"We had a tremendous team," Vander Werf recalled. "We had guys who could shoot lights out, but we needed a big man under the boards so we got Ron."

Kramer, of course, provided all the rebounds the team needed. But he also dumbfounded his new teammates with his overall athletic skills.

"Before the first game when he was warming up, we watched him dunk the ball standing flat-footed," Vander Werf recalled. "His vertical leap was unbelievable. And he was so quick for a man his size."

After Vander Werf was transferred to Milwaukee because of his job, he became acquainted with the Packers' team through Kramer. Years later, he ran into Hall of Fame linebacker Ray Nitschke in the Chicago airport.

"I remember Ray telling me that of all the great players the Packers had, Kramer was the best athlete," Vander Werf said. "There never was any question in my mind."

As soon as the basketball season ended at Michigan, Kramer changed shoes and slipped quickly into track. Despite being oversized at 6-foot-3 and 230 pounds, he was a talented high jumper who could regularly clear 6-foot-4. He also competed in the shot put and discus.

Just look at the body to understand why Kramer dominated every game he played. A champion shot putter at Michigan, he won nine varsity letters when freshmen were not eligible. (Reproduced by permission from Bentley Historical Library, University of Michigan)

"One of the most amazing sporting feats I ever witnessed didn't take place on the football field," said longtime friend Dick Scott.

It happened in the field house at Eastern Michigan University where Scott was going to school. Michigan was in for a track meet and Scott wanted to see his buddy.

"It was the first day after the basketball season," Scott said. "Kramer had just put away his gym shoes and now he was competing in track. He hadn't practiced one day and went out and won the shot put and high jump, and it wasn't even close. He hadn't even been with the team. That's the kind of athlete he was."

Track was not just a recreational sport for Kramer as it is for some football players. He relished the season as much as he did any of the sports he played.

"The thing about track is that it's head-to-head competition," he said. "It's you against the field, and you better be disciplined or someone will steal your shorts right off your ass. A lot of track is competing against yourself. You have to push yourself past a place you never dreamed you'd ever reach."

When he finished his final track meet in his senior season and awaited the NFL draft, Kramer was awarded his ninth varsity letter. He is one of only a handful of Michigan athletes to earn that distinction. And he did so during the time when freshmen were ineligible to compete.

Track provided an even richer reward to Kramer. Through track he developed a lifelong friendship with Michigan's legendary Don Canham. Canham was the track coach before moving on to become one of the most celebrated athletic directors in Michigan—and NCAA—history.

All Michigan athletes were impressed with the debonair Canham. He was only a dozen years older than most of the young men he coached, and he dressed like he walked off the pages of Gentleman's Quarterly. He wore white buck shoes and drove a Cadillac convertible.

"I think all the guys hoped to be like Don someday," Peg Canham said.

Like everyone else, Canham was impressed with Kramer's unique athletic ability. No one that big and that strong was supposed to be that pliable. Peg Canham believes that in many ways, the coach and his prodigy shared many similar characteristics.

"Don was rough around the edges, too," she said. "He was just more polished than Ron. They led different lifestyles. Ron was used to locker rooms and Don was used to boardrooms. Underneath, though, they were similar. They had this intense feeling to compete and succeed. Inside, they're both big teddy bears. Both are loyal and can cry at the drop of a hat."

Through the years, Canham often sought Kramer's perspective on various situations that arose within the football program.

Before Canham hired Bo Schembechler as football coach in 1968, he asked Kramer what he knew about the then relatively unknown. He told Canham he'd only met him a couple of times in Green Bay when Schembechler visited Vince Lombardi. Kramer was impressed with Schembechler's success at Miami of Ohio. The school had produced such successful coaches as Paul Brown and Ara Parseghian.

"He seems a little forceful," Kramer told Canham. "That's a good thing. You won't have to mess with him. If you give him control, he'll be better than anyone you can get."

Canham took a chance on the anonymous coach with the strange sounding name and was wise enough to stand back and let him run the football program.

When Schembechler moved to Ann Arbor, Kramer invited him to dinner.

"I told him I wouldn't get into his business unless he asked, but that he had all my support," Kramer said. "Obviously, he didn't call. He didn't need to. He turned out to be as good at his job as Canham was at his. Canham couldn't have made a better choice."

When Canham retired and the university was looking for a new athletic director, Kramer organized the Detroit group of former Michigan players and contacted the Chicago crew. The two groups were going to combine their influence to make sure Schembechler got the job.

"The president was talking about some guy from North Carolina," Kramer said. "I called the guy in Carolina and asked if he was crazy. I told him Schembechler is going to be the A.D. so save your time."

Schembechler, of course, ascended to the position of athletic director, and Kramer felt comfortable with his school's entire athletic program under Bo.

That's tradition. That's Kramer. First impressions and all.

7 *Kramer of Michigan*

Years before Bo Schembechler ever dreamed he would have the opportunity to be head football coach for the University of Michigan, he had his first encounter with Ron Kramer.

No words were exchanged. In fact, the two never really met. The occasion, obviously, left a lasting impression.

Until Bo died in 2006, based upon a friendship of both being "Michigan Men," they smiled about the incident that occurred in what seems to be another lifetime.

At the time, Bo was head coach for Miami (Ohio) University. Kramer had established himself as a legitimate star for the Green Bay Packers.

Jack Hecker, a member of Bo's staff, had a brother who was part of Vince Lombardi's Green Bay coaching staff. Through his brother, Hecker arranged for himself and Bo to visit the Packers' training camp in Wisconsin for a week before the start of another season.

Lombardi welcomed the two young, enthusiastic college coaches who were eager to tap into his wisdom and experience. Bo and Hecker were housed with the team in a dormitory on the campus of St. Norbert's University where the team trained.

They observed all the practices and studied Lombardi's techniques. They took notes. They shared meals with the team in the mess hall. More importantly, they got a firsthand look at what made Lombardi the master of the profession in which these two unknowns were trying to make their marks.

Bo was sitting next to Lombardi one evening when a pair of his Packers dramatically walked into the room fifteen minutes after the team had finished their meal.

It was Kramer and his mischievous sidekick, Paul Hornung—Green Bay's answer to Butch Cassidy and the Sundance Kid.

Anyone who knew the difference between a touchdown and a field goal was aware of this notoriously engaging pair. Kramer was the two-time All-American from Michigan who was redefining the role of the tight end position. Hornung was the "Golden Boy" from Notre Dame who had won the Heisman Trophy and the hearts of female fans across the country. His legend as a playboy made that of President John F. Kennedy look like it belonged to a high school sophomore.

With cigars hanging from their mouths, Kramer and Hornung slipped into the back of the room and attempted to get a meal before service was suspended.

"I slyly looked over at Vince," Bo said. "Man, he was pissed!"

One of the Packer rookies had been ordered by the veterans to stand on his chair and sing his college fight song. They wanted it loud so that the whole room could hear the words. Razing was a popular part of all football lore, particularly before the dawning of political correctness. The rookie was singing enthusiastically when Lombardi rose from his chair.

"Shut up!" Lombardi barked as he passed the nervous performer.

The quivering rookie instantly became mute as a mime. The room became suddenly silent. Bo's eyes were anxiously fixed on the furious coach as he cornered his miscreants.

"He lit into both of them with both barrels," Bo said. "'You will not go out drinking beer and come in here late,' he was shouting. He went on for a while, letting them have it from all sides."

When Lombardi finished, he walked by the rookie who was still standing obediently on his chair.

"Start singing," Lombardi instructed him softly.

It wasn't the first time, and certainly not the last, that Kramer and Hornung felt the wrath of their beloved coach.

"It didn't bother us," Kramer said. "We knew we had it coming. Bo didn't understand that we were used to that. We accepted it and respected Lombardi. Besides, Vince was wrong. We were drinking martinis the night before.

"Bo was the same way with his teams. Vince and Bo were very similar. Forceful. Great yellers. Both were disciplinarians. They're perfectionists and have only one thing in mind—football. They were passionate and they were not going to let anything stand in the way of building a winning team. Both were very smart."

Kramer appreciated the way both communicated. It wasn't so much the way both said things as it was what they had to say.

"I love people who can communicate exactly what's on their mind," Kramer said. "Vince and Bo were wonderful communicators. The reason they were so good is that they commanded respect. There are certain personalities that naturally command respect. They have a certain kind of energy, a certain kind of charisma. Call it whatever you want, both of them had it—on and off the field."

While coaching at Bowling Green, Bo saw Kramer play a game against Ohio State in Ann Arbor. Like everyone else who followed college football in the 1950s, Bo was amazed at Kramer's athleticism.

"He showed up and just flat out competed," Bo said. "He was big and strong. But he also was quick. He could move like a man much less his size. Even if someone didn't know football, you couldn't keep your eyes off him. He could have played in any era."

Characters like Kramer, however, only come around once in a lifetime.

"Sometimes Ron puts his foot in his mouth, but you have to love him," Bo said. "He's a very generous man. His heart is in the right place. He does more for charity than anyone will know."

For more than Kramer's athletic abilities, Schembechler admired his passion for the University of Michigan.

"Ron was a great player who enhanced his greatness to the university with his undying respect for the school," Bo said. "More than anyone I know, no player has shown as much respect to his school as Ron Kramer. I gave him his name—Kramer of Michigan."

8 *A Fitting Farewell*

"**W**hat are we going to do with Bennie?" the surreptitious voice whispered through Ron Kramer's phone.

"Where is he?" Kramer asked.

The voice belonged to a friend who also happened to be a funeral director.

"He's in the box," the voice replied.

Kramer told the voice to "hang on." He would be right over. There had always been a special relationship between Kramer and Bennie. Now that Bennie had died, Kramer had to do something special.

Bennie Oosterbaan was one of the early University of Michigan legends. First he made his mark as an all-around student athlete. He then went on to become a successful football coach at the school he loved only slightly less than his family. Like his protégé Kramer, Oosterbaan earned nine varsity letters for Michigan—three each in football, basketball, and baseball. Kramer did it in football, basketball, and track.

Oosterbaan was the school's first football player to win All-American honors three times. Kramer did it twice. Both played primarily at tight end. Each of their football numbers is retired.

Oosterbaan finished his storied playing career years before Kramer had even been born. The relationship they shared began when Kramer went to Michigan to play football under Coach Oosterbaan. Despite Oosterbaan's passing, Kramer still considers his relationship with his old coach very much alive.

"He's still with me," Kramer said. "I think about him all the time. It's impossible to forget anyone as sincere as Bennie. He taught me a lot that goes far beyond the football field. I owe him a lot."

Kramer and Bo Schembechler eulogized the former coach at the memorial service. Oosterbaan had survived the passing of his wife and son so a decision had to be made about the ashes of his remains.

The funeral director, a friend of Kramer, called for help.

"For about a week, I took Bennie everywhere I went," Kramer said. "I'd put him on the bar and tell the bartender to give me a couple of whiskey and waters—one for me and one for my friend Bennie. I'd tell the bartender Bennie was kind of dry. The bartender would look at me kind of funny. Then I'd tell him what was in the box. They always looked shocked. I took him here. I took him there. Bennie would have loved it. We had a special kind of friendship that's hard to explain."

Kramer wrestled with the situation of what to do with Bennie. Serendipitously, he was struck by an idea.

Suddenly it seemed so simple. Bennie had to be returned to all the places closest to his heart.

Alone, Kramer took the box of ashes and slowly traced a path around the campus that his mentor had traveled countless times before. Carefully, he sprinkled Bennie's ashes around the baseball field. He did the same around Yost Field House where Bennie had excelled in so many basketball games. He put some on the university golf course where Bennie loved to play.

Finally, Kramer went to the Big House. He placed some in the tunnel leading from the locker room to the field. Then he carefully spread some on the field that had defined Bennie's life. Kramer felt comfortable that his old coach would always be part of the Big House.

Kramer finished his mission by sprinkling ashes around the Oosterbaan Football Indoor Practice Building named in honor of his old coach.

Kramer was proud of his inspiration and confident Bennie would have felt the same way.

"This was everything he loved in life," Kramer explained. "Bennie absolutely loved the University of Michigan. He lived it … breathed it. He taught all of us how much it means and what an honor it is to represent the school on the athletic fields. He told us it was a special privilege that we will carry for our lifetimes."

Though their introduction was hardly memorable, Kramer's devotion to Oosterbaan began almost immediately after arriving as a freshman football recruit. While a senior at East Detroit High

School, Kramer was taken to a Michigan game by Bill Mazur and Johnny Green. The two introduced him to the coach.

"Hi ... how are you?" the mild-mannered coach greeted Kramer. "Hope you come here."

Kramer still smiles at the low-key introduction.

"That was it," Kramer said. "No sales pitch, no nothing. He loved Michigan so much he never dreamed he had to sell it to anyone."

For football and basketball, Kramer had his pick of any school in the country. Recruiting in the 1950s, however, was not the cutthroat business it has evolved into today. Kramer already had decided to attend the University of Michigan. He didn't need a sales pitch even from its most passionate promoter.

Kramer's uncanny athletic abilities, no doubt, led to Oosterbaan's admiration.

"I could do anything he could ... only better," Kramer said.

But the relationship transcended athletic superiority.

"Bennie had a son who died when he was quite young," said Tom Maentz who played opposite end of Kramer. "He died a few years before we came on the scene. I think Bennie always had a feeling that Ron was a surrogate son. Almost from the day we hit the campus, he took Ron under his wing. They shared a lot of mutual respect. Bennie never favored him at the expense of other players, but you could sense there was something special between the two."

During the off-seasons while Kramer played for the Green Bay Packers and Detroit Lions, he regularly drove to Ann Arbor simply to visit his old coach. When he retired from football, the visits continued. When Bennie became ill, the visits became more frequent. He had visited Oosterbaan the day he died.

"I'm not going to make it this time, Krames," Kramer recalls Oosterbaan telling him that afternoon.

Kramer did his best not to believe him. As usual, though, the old coach was right.

"I used to take my wives, my girlfriends, even my dogs when I went to visit," Kramer said. "Bennie loved it when I'd bring a pretty girl to the house."

Kramer was careful to keep the visits personal and quiet. No one else needed to know. Bennie and Kramer both preferred it this way.

"Those visits speak volumes about the character of Ron

Kramer," observed former Michigan tackle Jim Brandstatter. "He was a virile ex-athlete and businessman who was in demand. He also had a job that kept him busy all the time. Yet he always found time to drive from Detroit to Ann Arbor just to spend time with his elderly coach. No one knew about it. Only those two.

"Think about how many people can't find time to visit parents living in a nursing home. That says more about Ron Kramer than anything he did as an athlete. As great as he was, all he did for Bennie was greater."

At the football banquet following the 1956 season, Oosterbaan retired number 87, which Kramer had so marvelously distinguished.

"At the time I was dumbfounded," Kramer said. "I didn't know what to say. I didn't really know what retiring a number meant. And besides, I was preparing for the basketball season. Now that I'm old, I understand the significance of it. I owe it all to Bennie."

Kramer found a way to return the honor to his old coach. Bennie would be proud.

9   *A Legend of Its Own*

"Kramer of Michigan?" growled the voice on the telephone line.

The growl sounded familiar, but for a moment Ron Kramer was confused.

"Yeah," he answered. "Who's this?"

There was a slight pause.

"This is Schembechler—coach of Michigan," the voice replied. "Now where were those apples like you brought last week?"

It was a Wednesday evening in October 1987. On the previous Wednesday, Kramer had delivered a couple of bushels of apples for the football players and coaches to enjoy after a vigorous practice.

"You brought them last Wednesday and we won on Saturday," Schembechler continued. "Now how come they're not here today?"

The two continued their banter for a while until Schembechler told him he was preparing for a game and had work to do.

"You've got to bring those apples," the coach again barked. "And don't forget that apple juice."

Kramer corrected him by saying it was cider.

"Yeah, cider," the coach growled again. "Now don't forget it."

That was the official start of Kramer's weekly autumn apple football run. Now, twenty years later, the route has grown to proportions Kramer never dreamed it would.

The tradition actually began somewhere in the 1940s when a Michigan football fanatic, known only as Mr. Chestnut, used to deliver two or three bushels of apples to practice each Wednesday. The tradition carried into the 1950s and ceased with the death of friendly Mr. Chestnut.

"Man, I used to love those apples," Kramer was salivating as he recalled. "I used to devour them ... crunch, crunch, crunch. I'd run those sprints to the apples so fast after practice. I always made sure I was the first one there."

After Kramer moved to just outside of Fenton in 1987, he remembered the city also had been home to Mr. Chestnut. The city and surrounding area are rich with apple orchards.

"I was going to Ann Arbor one day," Kramer said. "I don't know why the idea struck me, but I just decided to bring some apples for the boys."

And he's done so ever since.

Shortly after the apple tradition had been revitalized, one of Michigan's all-time great receivers got his introduction to Kramer. Anthony Carter asked a teammate who the "old guy with the apples" was.

Equipment Manager Jon Falk overheard the question. He quickly instructed Carter to look around the field and pick out the player wearing number 87.

The young man did as instructed. After a fruitless search, he told Falk that he did not see number 87 anywhere.

"And you never will!" Falk shouted. "That's because it belongs to HIM! That's Ron Kramer. Kramer of Michigan. No one will ever wear that number again."

Kramer decided to add to the tradition of apples. He expanded his route to the athletic offices. Then came the ticket office. Next came the marketing office. His last addition was the office of University President Mary Sue Coleman.

"That's my girl," Kramer said. "I just drop in and say hello to everybody. All the girls there love me. I don't think it's for my looks. I'm pretty sure it's for my apples."

Coleman begs to differ with the always congenial Kramer. She is "touched" by the weekly visits that run throughout the football season.

"Of course, we appreciate the apples," Coleman said. "They're delicious. But everyone in the office looks forward to his visits even more than for the apples. Good times or bad times, he's always so upbeat and concerned about the team. He makes everyone on the staff take a breath and smile."

Coleman said she tires of fair weather fans who criticize the coach, the team, or university at the first sign of adversity.

"Ron understands that we're in this for the long haul, and his loyalty never wavers," she said.

Neither does his passion and commitment to the university.

"Ron is one of our living traditions," Coleman said. "He's the embodiment of the passion which people feel about Michigan football. I can't imagine a better friend of Michigan football."

Former University of Michigan Regent Neal Nielsen calls Kramer "an ambassador to the institution."

"He's an icon in the athletic world," said Nielsen, who also serves as Kramer's attorney. "He's one of those few people who have excelled at the highest level of sports and also has been a leader in the life he's led. He's maintained dignity in an environment that can be extremely testing. There's no braggadocio with Ron. He's done it through his actions."

Bruce Madej is Michigan's longtime associate athletic director in charge of media relations. Over the years, he has witnessed countless examples of Kramer's dedication to his alma mater.

"He can't say no when it comes to something that will benefit the university, particularly the football program," Madej said.

About ten years ago, Kramer showed up at an annual golf tournament that raises money for the athletic scholarship fund. He was not going to play because he was scheduled for knee surgery the following morning. Instead, he planned to ride a cart around the course and visit with various supporters of the event.

It didn't happen. At the last moment, sensing he could raise a few more dollars for the fund, Kramer decided to play.

Kramer joined the foursome of Madej, Bo Schembechler, then athletic director Joe Roberson, and tournament coordinator Al Glick.

"I was riding with Bo and we couldn't believe what we were seeing," Madej said. "Kramer could hardly walk and he was knocking the ball out of sight. Bo said he'd never seen such a competitor."

Glick remembers watching Kramer perform on Saturdays in the Big House.

"I specifically remember one play against Michigan State when he blocked a punt," Glick said. "It must have shot at least twenty feet up into the air. Ron waited for it to start falling, then jumped up over everyone to snag it and take it into the end zone for a touchdown. He had such God-given talent."

On the final hole of the golf outing, there was a substantial wager within the group. Kramer had trouble simply getting in and out of the cart. Nevertheless, he found himself on the green with a thirty-foot birdie putt.

"He sank that putt as if a pro had done it," Madej marveled.

"He took his winnings and promptly donated it to the scholarship fund."

The gesture was hardly surprising to Madej who had become familiar with Kramer's generosity over the years.

"Ask Ron Kramer to do something for the university and no one jumps faster," Madej said. "No former player is more generous. He's a throwback. He's one of the toughest SOBs you'll ever meet."

Kramer established another unofficial record on the University of Michigan Golf Course and this one had absolutely nothing to do with golf.

The course serves as a giant parking facility for Michigan home football games. For noon kickoffs, tailgating often starts just about the time the sun is rising for another colorful autumn day.

As might be expected, Kramer is a hit at any tailgate party he happens to visit.

The indoor clubhouse lavatory facilities, however, are at a premium. As lines threatened to run out the door, people not even familiar with Kramer would gain access simply by saying: "I'm with Kramer." The custodian finally had "I'm with Kramer" badges made to help alleviate the situation.

"It never really worked," Kramer laughed. "A few weeks later, it seemed like everybody showed up wearing an 'I'm with Kramer' badge."

Kramer keeps his pinned to the wall in his office. His identity is quite obvious.

Michigan is a university that is founded upon tradition. It's home to such football legends as Fielding H. Yost, Fritz Crisler, Bennie Oosterbaan, Bo Schembechler, President Gerald R. Ford, Tom Harmon, and a litany of luminaries that make the history books look as if Michigan had invented the game.

Michigan has more football victories than any school in the country. It plays in the Big House, the largest stadium in the land. "The Victors" is the most recognized college fight song. There's the game for the "Little Brown Jug" with Minnesota. Every school has traditional football rivalries. None, however, is more celebrated than the annual clash between Michigan and Ohio State.

It may not rank with such celebrated traditions, but Kramer with his apples adds to the romance of autumn in Ann Arbor.

"It's just a tiny blip on the radar screen compared to all of those other things," said former player Jim Brandstatter. "But think about it for a moment. What other former great athlete who's older now and a little hunched over is going to show up every Wednesday of the football season delivering apples to the team because that's the way it was when he played? And then walk into the president's office with a bushel of apples and get away with it? But that's who he is and everybody loves him because he's so friendly.

"That says everything you need to know about his character and how much the university means to Ron Kramer."

Kramer of Michigan. Football legend ... and Wednesday afternoon apple man.

10   *What's Wrong with Green Bay?*

Maybe the admiration for his father's relentless work ethic had something to do with it. For a fleeting moment, though, Ron Kramer thought about entering the normal work force and foregoing professional football after graduating from the University of Michigan in 1957.

Kramer loved all the games that had defined his life since the first time he put any kind of ball in his hand. He mastered all of them with the ease of a computer geek logging on to the internet. He appreciated the discipline the games demanded. He knew what it took to be regarded as one of the nation's best athletes.

Sports are coldly fickle, though. Particularly one as violent as professional football. One careless move or one unsuspected crunching collision, and even the brightest future can fizzle like a wet Fourth of July sparkler.

John Kramer had taught his son that nothing is more critical to any young man contemplating having a family than the security of a reliable job. John had imparted that wisdom through words and punctuated it with his own tireless work ethic.

Ron was the first in the Kramer family ever to have attended a university. Kramer was proud of the degree he had earned in four years at one of the nation's leading academic institutions. He also was determined not to let his well-earned once-in-a-lifetime opportunity slip away.

So despite being the number one draft choice of the Green Bay Packers, Kramer decided to investigate various possibilities before committing to his future.

Because his father had spent a lifetime working for Chevrolet, the first option seemed obvious. Kramer arranged for an interview with the booming auto company, General Motors. This had nothing to do with the forge plant where his father had sweat for so many years. John's college graduate, All-American football playing son had earned the opportunity to meet with the comptroller of the company, Fred Frazer.

"The guy was great," Kramer recalled. "He was a big Michigan fan. He also said he knew about my dad."

The highly placed executive asked what Kramer wanted to do with his future.

"I told him I had a chance to play for the Packers," Kramer said. "I told him I was thinking about giving it a shot."

The gentle comptroller courteously stopped Kramer from saying another word.

"Don't think about it," he said. "Go out and give it a try. If things don't work out, you come back and we'll work something out."

The decision was made. Kramer was ready for the first step of his new life.

Playing in the National Football League is every young boy's fantasy. Getting the opportunity to play as a team's number one draft choice is a bold dream that only the fearless dare.

But Green Bay in 1957? The Packers' highlight films could have been used as "how not to play the game" lessons for aspiring high school and collegiate wannabes. In 1956, the Packers posted a woeful 4-8 record. They regressed to 3-9 in 1957. In 1958, they countered 10 losses with one victory and one tie.

It wasn't merely the mediocrity on the field that made the franchise as appealing as a popsicle in January for highly decorated All-Americans hungry to make a mark under the bright lights of one of the big cities in the league.

The Packers simply didn't play under any bright lights. Not merely in distance, Green Bay was light years from New York or Chicago or Los Angeles. Even the industrial giants of Detroit and Cleveland looked cosmopolitan compared to the speck on the Wisconsin map called Green Bay.

Green Bay was tabbed as the "Siberia of the NFL" by Jim Murray, the late celebrated sports columnist of the *Los Angeles Times*. He once wrote that "mackinaws were considered formal wear in the city that the Packers called home."

It has grown and become far more gentrified since Vince Lombardi's teams officially put the city on the world-wide sporting map. Nevertheless, Green Bay was, and still remains, the smallest market in the NFL. And to top it off, the Packers had been awful before the arrival of Lombardi. They were so bad, in fact, that they earned the dubious distinction of getting the bonus pick in the 1957 draft. In those days, the team with the worst record in the previous season received a selection before the start of the regular player draft.

Jack Vainisi was a shrewd judge of football talent, however. Before Lombardi arrived, the director of player personnel made sure the cupboards were stocked well enough with talent for the new coach to at least have a chance at making his system work.

With the bonus pick, the Packers wisely chose Notre Dame's Paul Hornung who actually considered playing a year in Canada before he could move to another more "civilized" franchise.[1] Hornung actually wanted to play for the Chicago Bears. The Chicago Cardinals had tied the Packers for the worst record in 1956. The Packers won a coin flip and because his mother desired him to stay in the United States, Hornung was on his way to Green Bay.[2] With the first pick of the regular round, the Packers chose the University of Michigan's Ron Kramer.

It could arguably be stated this was one of the best drafts in history for any particular franchise.

Fritz Crisler, the legendary former coach and athletic director for the University of Michigan, handled contract negotiations for Kramer. Crisler was considered to be one of the most astute practitioners of all phases of the game. He was committed to secure a guaranteed future for the Michigan prodigy.

Because Kramer was part of the Air Force ROTC program at Michigan, he faced the distinct possibility of military service. In addition to a $15,000 annual base salary, Crisler negotiated a deal in which Kramer would receive an additional $3,000 a year for three straight years regardless of whether he was with the Packers or in the service.

Some pundits joked Kramer would fare better in the service. Unlike the Packers, at least the military supplied weapons to fight a war.

For Kramer, where he played really didn't matter. Once he decided to play professionally, he was committed to showcasing and

---

[1] Hornung, *Golden Boy*, p. 60.
[2] Ibid., p. 60.

enhancing the skills that made him one of the most coveted athletes on the face of the planet.

Kramer and Hornung not only complemented each other as players, their mischievous personalities led to a lifelong friendship that remains as strong today as when they ruled the field.

They had already formed a friendship while making a few college recruiting visits as high school seniors. They spent time together making the rounds as members of the consensus All-American team in the late fall of 1956. While playing in the College All-Star Game in August 1957, the two agreed to drive together from Chicago to report to the Packers' training camp.

"Hornung was beautiful," Kramer recalled. "I thought I had seen it all when we were in New York for an appearance on the Ed Sullivan Show and he made a run at Kim Novak.

"Now, when we arrived at the training camp, there was a girl waiting for him as soon as he got out of the car."

The girl was—according to Kramer's generous recollection—somewhat of a mix between Ray Nitschke and Henry Jordan. The Packers already were familiar with Hornung's playboy reputation and couldn't wait to roast their new supposed franchise savior.

While at Notre Dame, Hornung received a massive amount of fan mail, particularly letters that arrived in perfumed envelopes. Between football, class work, and various other "extracurricular activities," Hornung had neither time nor interest to respond. Hornung hired a friend to reply to as many letters as possible. Apparently the friend wrote to the young lady that Hornung would be anxious to meet her at training camp.[3]

Unbeknownst to all, that particular day signaled the infancy of a colorful new era in sports that would transcend the boundaries of sleepy, little Green Bay, both on and off the field.

The legends of all those players—and particularly Vince Lombardi—were about to explode across the country with deafening thunder.

Kramer may have earned more money working for a corporation like General Motors. But he would have missed the ride of a lifetime.

And fans would have missed one of the best tight ends ever to have played the game.

---

[3]Ibid., p. 63.

11 *Pain Is the Price*

Ron Kramer prefers to laugh at himself rather than to mope in self-pity.

"Look at me," he cracks as he pulls himself from the well-worn recliner that is the best box seat for any football game television has to offer. "I used to be 6-foot-3, maybe 6-4. If I get any shorter now, I'll be a pygmy."

The back is hunched over, but the shoulders remain wide and strong as two-by-fours. Surgical scars stripe wide patches of his flesh with the ruts and ridges of a country back road.

His head is bald, his legs are bowed, and his fingers are bent. The body pays a painful price from too many collisions with other human condominiums dressed in full football gear from so many years ago. Particularly sadistic vampires posing as NFL linebackers on Sundays.

Still, his eyes sparkle with an unmistakable glint of mischief and confidence. The look never wavers, never wanes. It remains defiantly young and signals the soul of the truly gifted champion.

"I never abused my body," Kramer carefully makes the distinction. "I used it. I never worried about what might happen down the line. I played for the day—the way the game's supposed to be played. I have no regrets. I can handle all of it. I deal with the moment."

Kramer smiles when he recalls his mother's early warnings about playing sports.

"When I first started playing she worried that I might get hurt," he said. "After seeing me play in a few games, she always warned me not to hurt the other boys."

Pain is the currency for success in the NFL. Almost every

player has to meet the price. Even the most gifted. Kramer certainly has paid his dues.

"Nobody walks away from the game for free," Kramer says matter-of-factly. "If you've been there and done things right, you're going to hurt. I never thought about it when I played and I don't complain about it now. It's part of the game."

With eighteen surgeries under his belt, Kramer is a walking medical encyclopedia that ought to be required reading for every promising physician. His litany of injuries resulted in five knee surgeries (including two new knees), three shoulder surgeries (including both shoulders), one new hip, and a ruptured Achilles tendon. The preceding list does not include countless sprained ankles, broken fingers, and "little nicks like that." He has also had heart surgery (carotid artery and four arterial stents, two each from a pair of procedures).

"I looked at myself the other day to see how many cuts I really have over my body," he smiled. "I thought I was really knocking the hell out of people. I guess a few of them got to me, too. When I die, instead of putting me in a graveyard, they're going to put my body in a junkyard, with all the metal and plastic parts in me."

Kramer's most serious injury occurred in his rookie season and threatened to end his promising career even before it had a chance to blossom.

It happened in the next to last game of the season when the Packers were being routed by the Los Angeles Rams. Kramer went up for a pass and was cut off his feet at the knees on a clean hit by a diving safety.

Crrrrr-unch!

Kramer managed to hang on to the ball. Even before struggling to his feet, he realized something was seriously wrong. He hobbled to the sideline and told the trainer he felt there was a knife stuck inside his leg. He thought the leg was ready to crack off right around the knee.

The trainer quickly taped it and Kramer limped back on to the field. Those were the days when a rookie couldn't afford to get hurt. Miss a few plays and the epitaph on his playing career might read: "He had great potential."

The swelling was immediate and the pain too severe for more than one last play. Kramer's year ended in a flash of agony. He finished his rookie season with twenty-eight receptions, good for a twelve-yard average, in eleven games.

Even more impressive was his ability to knock defenders into the second row of the grandstand. He had established himself as a worthy number one draft choice. The fans in Green Bay loved his style of controlled mayhem. Suddenly his future was put on hold.

Post-game X-rays did not reveal the severity of the injury. Kramer's self-prescribed pain reliever of a table full of martinis helped get him through the night.

"We were in Los Angeles," he reasoned. "We had to go out on the street. No dancing with the glass on my head that night, though."

By morning, the knee had swelled to an ugly disproportion. He was taken to the hospital where further X-rays revealed a break at the crest of the tibia. He was placed in a cast that ran from hip to toe.

Two months later, the cast was removed but the pain would not subside. Kramer decided to visit Dr. Carl Badgley, a renowned surgeon and head of orthopedics at the University of Michigan Hospital.

Dr. Badgley performed exploratory surgery. Under local anesthetic, Kramer still can hear the doctor's voice.

"Oh my God ... we've got problems," the doctor remarked. "We'll operate tomorrow."

The problems were far more serious than Kramer had imagined. Not only had he broken the tibia, he also had torn the interior collateral ligament and the anterior and posterior cruciate ligaments. Dr. Badgley told him surgery would help him to mend. But the prognosis was not quite so promising.

"He told me I would never play football again," Kramer said. "Those are words an athlete never forgets."

Kramer, of course, was stunned, but stubborn enough not to accept surrender. He simply needed time to figure how to resolve this unexpected challenge.

"Sure, I had fear that I might never play again," he said. "When a doctor says something like that, any athlete with half a brain would have to be concerned."

That job offer he had at Chevrolet now didn't seem to look so bad.

After recovering from surgery, Kramer went to Green Bay. He tried to run pass patterns to convince the Packers—and more importantly himself—that he could still play.

The performance wasn't pretty.

"I wasn't too sharp," Kramer admitted. "I looked like a peg-legged pirate trying to chase a parrot around a ship."

Those were the days when formal team rehabilitation programs weren't even a pipe dream. Once a season ended, a player was left to rehabilitate and train on his own.

So he devised his own rehab program demanding the same discipline he had applied to every game or any other challenge.

He bought a set of weights and tortured himself like a professional lifter. More importantly, he purchased a separate one-hundred-pound weight that he carried wherever he traveled. Each day, as religiously as making his bed in the morning, he kicked the weight two thousand times. One thousand times with the right leg. One thousand times with the left.

Slowly, he could feel the pain subside and strength seep back into the muscles. He was determined to return for the 1958 season.

There suddenly appeared some unexpected additional rehab time, however. Uncle Sam had come knocking.

Kramer had served in the ROTC at the University of Michigan. After having failed three physical exams to enter the Air Force flight school because of his injury, he was cleared for regular active duty. He declined an invitation to play military football because of his knee and was assigned to a desk job in Washington, D.C.

After serving one year, he was honorably discharged from active duty. He would be back in time for the 1959 season.

"The rehab I did on my knee is one of my proudest accomplishments," Kramer claims without hesitation. "I was never supposed to play again. No athlete wants to go out like that. I was fortunate, but I know how hard I worked. Maybe the hardest of my life. That was discipline, baby. Without it, I never would have made it."

When he returned in 1959, though, the Packers were not the same. The biggest change, of course, was Green Bay's third new head coach in three years.

Kramer played his rookie season under Lisle Blackbourn. Kramer was sidelined for Ray "Scooter" McLean's three shades of ugly 1958 season when the Packers posted an ignominious 1-10-1 record. His return in 1959 coincided with the first steps of Green Bay's march toward sports immortality.

Vince Lombardi had arrived.

Despite his tireless rehabilitation, Kramer was merely a ghost of the player who had brought so much potential to the frozen land of the north. No amount of workouts and rehabilitation can compensate for any athlete sitting out a whole season.

"You have doubts," Kramer admitted. "Nothing improves an athlete more than playing experience. Nothing makes you wonder more if you'll ever play again than sitting on your ass for a year."

After his military discharge, Kramer reported to the Packers with one week of training left before the start of the 1959 season.

The rehab had worked. Kramer was running pass patterns again. Playing against behemoths dressed in full football gear and breaking five-seconds in the forty-yard dash, however, was a lot different than lifting or kicking weights.

Kramer pushed himself through a grueling ninety minutes of running pass patterns. He avoided visiting the trainer's room after practice.

"Lombardi didn't really care to see players in that room," Kramer said. "It didn't matter who they were."

Instead, he returned to the room he was sharing with Max McGee and iced his knee like a frozen martini. Only this time, there would be no dancing.

"I didn't want anyone to know," Kramer said. "That knee would swell up like a pregnant walrus."

Nevertheless, Kramer scraped through the 1959 and 1960 seasons although his playing time was sparse and limited primarily to duty on the special teams.

The world had turned upside down on one of football's most gifted natural athletes. What had always come so naturally now seemed impossible to reach.

"I was a mess," Kramer admitted. "I had ulcers. I was drinking milk and taking pills. I quit drinking and smoking and dropped to 210 pounds. I felt like I was from Auschwitz. I was like Charles Atlas in that old ad where the guy gets sand kicked into his face. It was unbelievable. I was a sick son of a bitch."

Something else was missing. The mental toughness he had always been able to turn on like a light switch wasn't quite as crisp.

"I didn't know what the hell going on," he said. "I knew it wasn't the real me. I just didn't know what the hell to do about it."

He knew he had to do something, though, and he had to do it quickly. First, he got a little help from one of his best friends.

12 *Attitude Adjustment*

It was a typical frigid Green Bay night in late November 1960. Ron Kramer and Paul Hornung decided it was a perfect evening to take the ladies to dinner. Kramer and his wife, Nancy, were in the front seat of his Oldsmobile convertible. Hornung was comfortably seated in the middle of the back seat with a beautiful woman on either side.

"That was his idea of a double date," Kramer cracked. "One girl for each arm."

They drove to one of their favorite restaurants. During dinner, Kramer, uncharacteristically, was sipping Coke. Hornung and the three ladies were having a gay time generously pouring themselves several glasses of champagne.

It was obvious to all—Kramer was in no mood to be the life of the party. As the evening wore on and tongues became looser, Hornung decided to dish out some tough love to his best friend.

"You big, dumb son of a bitch," Hornung told Kramer. "What's wrong with you? You gotta get your shit together. You know what you can do. I know what you can do. Everybody knows what you can do. Now get your ass in gear and do it. We're gonna need you next year."

Only a couple of games were left in the season. The Packers went on to win the conference title with an 8-4 record. They lost, 17–13, to the Eagles in the championship game in Philadelphia.

In spite of the loss, Green Bay fans looked eagerly toward the next season. Vince Lombardi had started the great Green Bay turnaround. The Packers reached the championship game in just Lombardi's second season. In Lombardi's first year in 1959, the Packers tied for third place with a 7-5 record. It marked their first winning season since 1947, when they finished 6-5-1.

Kramer appeared in all twelve regular season games in 1959 and 1960, mostly on special teams. He didn't catch one pass in 1959 and grabbed only four for fifty-five yards in 1960.

Kramer had suffered through a series of physical injuries. The lack of physical contact and real game experience, though, did more damage to his psyche than the injuries did to his body.

"When an athlete doubts his confidence, he's in big trouble," Kramer admitted.

Lombardi, Hornung, and all of the Packers were confident, however, the best was yet to come for Kramer. All he had to do now was to convince himself.

"Take a drink of champagne," Hornung commanded his friend. "Let's get it going."

Kramer obliged. Then they all took another … and another … and another until the waiter finally told them it was 2 a.m. and the place was ready to close.

No problem for the merry quintet. They piled into Kramer's Oldsmobile convertible and the suddenly jovial tight end quickly put the top down.

"It was so cold that it couldn't get colder," Kramer recalled. "It didn't matter if the top was up or down."

No one noticed as they sang their way to an all-night Italian restaurant where they finished the evening eating pizza and spaghetti. It was after four o'clock when Kramer pulled up to his house. Hornung and his two friends for the evening already had decided to spend the night there.

At eight in the morning, Kramer had the coffee brewed for his wife and three guests who stumbled to the table nursing hangovers the size of Wisconsin.

"I felt pretty damn good," Kramer said. "I told myself I've got to kick myself in the ass and get my head back into this."

Certainly a night on the town—even one in cozy Green Bay—is not an elixir for a stalled career. It just happened to be a start. The punctuation mark came soon after the season ended, when Kramer was summoned to Lombardi's office.

The coach's message came without the trimmings of champagne, spaghetti, or the quaintness of a freezing Green Bay evening. It was succinct and clear. Most would call it an ultimatum. But the wise coach already had determined Kramer was the type that welcomes a challenge he simply can't refuse.

"We can't pay you as much as you're making for what you're giving us," Lombardi flatly told him. "I think you're better than what you've shown. I have faith in you. You're my tight end when you come back next season. I think you can play this position as I see how it has to be played. Now it's up to you to make it happen."

The tight end position, at the time, belonged to Gary Knafelc. A decent receiver, Knafelc was like a size-nine foot trying to fill a size-twelve shoe. He worked hard, had good hands, ran good passing routes, and could catch the ball. He simply lacked the size, strength, and quickness Kramer naturally possessed.

Lombardi's vision of Kramer playing tight end was significantly different from what was expected of the position at the time.

Most tight ends were an extension of the offensive line. Their primary mission was to block and open holes for running backs or protect the quarterback from having his head knocked down into his shoulder pads. Often they were called upon to team with a tackle and double up on a rusher.

Kramer could do all that and so much more. He was the perfect specimen to fill the role Lombardi needed to complete his vision of the famous Packer sweep that became the team's trademark.

Kramer had the hands to catch any pass within radar distance. He was powerful enough to go up the middle to snag a pass in the middle of traffic and quick enough to outrun linebackers and even some safeties for extra yards.

More importantly was his ability to block. The position, as Lombardi envisioned, wasn't designed merely for Kramer to double up a defender. He had the size, strength, and speed to take on a defender single-handedly.

"The difference between Ron and the other tight ends was his ability to catch a pass and move with the ball," said linebacker Mike Lucci, who played against him while with the Cleveland Browns. "He was the best tight end blocker around and you still had to account for him on every play."

With that luxury, Lombardi felt he could run his offense as if he had twelve men on the field. Kramer had defined what would be expected of every good future tight end.

Now it was up to Kramer to complete Lombardi's vision.

"In my opinion, Ron Kramer was the best tight end that ever played the game," said Fuzzy Thurston, the left guard on the celebrated Green Bay line.

"He could do everything. Block. Catch passes. Anything the play called for. He had the biggest hands you ever saw. Mammoth. They were powerful, but soft enough for catching passes.

"If somebody was going to write a book about what a tight end is supposed to do, he'd use Ron Kramer as a model. He would have made the Hall of Fame if he hadn't had those bad legs."

Quarterback Bart Starr felt safe behind the Green Bay line and didn't worry about a defender turning the corner on Kramer. He always felt comfortable throwing the ball to his favorite tight end.

"He had great, soft hands," Starr remarked. "He was big and strong, but had those soft hands. I felt very confident throwing to him."

The two still enjoy teasing each other whenever they are together.

"Bart will always say, 'How come you only caught four passes in such and such game,'" Kramer chuckled. "I tell him because he only threw it to me four times."

It is Kramer's all-around talent that remains very much alive in Starr's memory.

"I believe Ron could have played almost anywhere on the field," Starr said. "He was a tight end with a linebacker's tenacity. He was aggressive and loved to block. He also ran precise pass routes. I believe if there had been injuries, he could have flip-flopped and played on defense. He was that great an athlete."

Kramer didn't betray the confidence Lombardi showed in him. He seized the opportunity like a two-foot "gimme" putt in a hundred-dollar golf game. He started all fourteen regular season games in 1961. He caught thirty-five passes for 559 yards and scored four touchdowns.

In the 37–0 championship game rout of the New York Giants, Kramer played what many experts tabbed as the "perfect tight end game."

Some believed he deserved the Most Valuable Player award that went to his best pal, Hornung.

More important than all the statistics and numbers he produced, Kramer added presence to the position on the field.

"He just had such a tremendous understanding of everything that was going on around him on every play," Thurston said. "That makes it so much easier for every other guy out there to do his job. You never had to worry if Ron was going to get his assignment done. It got done ... and got done damn good."

The challenge Lombardi threw at Kramer obviously paid dividends for the whole team. That was the essence of Lombardi's brilliance. He could pick the player to leave alone and the one who thrived on a challenge.

Wide receiver Max McGee became intimately familiar with Lombardi's psychological war games.

"Lombardi could read his players so well," McGee said. "He knew which ones to chew out and which ones to leave alone. I kept getting caught for being out after curfew. He would rip my ass in front of the players. We wouldn't talk to each other for a few days. Then before the game, he'd come up and say, 'I had to do it, Max, to make sure everyone is moving in the right direction.' It was fine. I understood. You certainly can't argue with the results."

Kramer's response to the challenge Lombardi issued solidified their relationship.

"I think that's why he respected me," Kramer said. "He told me what he expected from me and I came back and did everything he wanted.

"It's hard for someone to understand what goes through the mind of an athlete who's had to sit out a year. It doesn't matter who they are. There are doubts. You have to whip them or they're going to eat your ass like a starving coyote. Lombardi knew how to lick it. We all owe everything to that man."

It took a long time and his career had to endure several unexpected turns along the way. But perseverance paid off for both Kramer and the Packers.

There's a difference between being bull-headed in the face of hopelessness and unyielding when there's at least a glimmer of hope.

"You have to recognize an opportunity and then make the most of it," Kramer said. "You can't do it without discipline."

13   *The Legend of Lombardi*

Vince Lombardi would have bristled at the notion. His appreciation of history and commitment to humanity simply wouldn't allow
him to entertain the suggestion. Not for a nanosecond.

While some Lombardi biographers stop just short of
apotheosizing him, the old coach would have laughed at the
hagiographic attempt. He might likely have told anyone wise
enough to listen that there are no heroes in sports, let alone saints.

Heroes are the guys buried in Arlington Cemetery. Their
contribution to history is always remembered. Their identities,
nevertheless, remain obscure.

Heroes are the brave men and women who risked or sacrificed
their lives helping the victims of that satanic September 11. Their
lone request in return is that such an atrocity never be allowed to
happen again.

The limelight of sports is an anathema to heroes. They thrive
more peacefully in the shade of anonymity.

Sports, however, are a fertile field for producing colorful
characters. The people that create memories passed from one
generation to the next. They're good for the sport and good for
community spirit. Just don't mistake them for heroes. They're only
playing a game.

Once in a lifetime, though, a magnanimous figure arises with a
gift that actually transcends the fields of play to influence the lives
of almost everyone he touches.

These guys are different. Their presence is more easily felt than
explained. To them, character and integrity win as many games as
pure physical talent.

Lombardi was no hero and certainly not a saint. He was,
instead, a leader and role model. That very special kind of leader

who believed life lived without purpose and commitment is no life at all. Only through discipline can all challenges be met.

Lombardi did not only preach the message. He lived it and breathed it into all the people he touched.

He may not have been a hero, but he certainly was a MAN!

Lombardi was one of those precious few whose shadow today is just as sweeping as it was when he was shouting and pacing the sidelines of football fields across America.

"No doubt about it," Ron Kramer said. "Not one day goes by when I don't think about him. He's part of my life and always will be. Anyone that ever knew him still carries a piece of his spirit.

"Guys like him are once in a lifetime. They change everything around them. To say that I was privileged to have played for Vince Lombardi is one of the proudest accomplishments of my life."

Lombardi was hired by the Packers to resuscitate a gasping franchise. He arrived with a vision for making the Packers a champion and wasted no time putting it to work.

Before Lombardi's first team posted a 7-5 record in 1959, the Packers hadn't finished above .500 since 1947 when they finished at 6-5-1. No Lombardi Packers team finished below .500.

In 1960, he led the team to a conference crown. In 1961 and 1962, the Packers marched to two straight NFL championships. Before

Even taking a Green Bay Packers team picture could be fun in 1962 after the team won the NFL championship the previous season.

he left Green Bay, the Packers won three more championships, including the first two Super Bowls.

"He had a singleness of purpose that I had never seen before," wide receiver Max McGee said. "He instilled that into all of us."

Lombardi's vision stretched far beyond the Xs and Os of a playbook. He believed that a champion evolves from the inside out. No amount of physical talent can compensate for a lack of character, integrity, discipline, and tireless work ethic.

New York Giants' owner Wellington Mara first became acquainted with Lombardi when the coach was an assistant at West Point. Mara hired Lombardi as an assistant for the Giants and was instrumental in getting him the job at Green Bay.

Mara was impressed by Lombardi's single-mindedness for the game. He was particularly moved, however, by the passion of the man who believed the formula for perfection was discipline and disdain for surrender.

"He could have been president," Mara said. "Or he could have been the pope. He had the zeal of a missionary."[4]

"He was more than just a football coach," Kramer said. "He was a teacher. He was a psychologist. He was a little bit of a con man and a little bit of a priest. He believed that to be truly successful, you had to develop the whole person. You can have all the talent in the world, but if you don't have discipline, character, and integrity, you can't be a champion. Not for the long run. That's true for any profession. Anyone who played for him carries what he taught for the rest of their lives."

At the time Kramer returned from his service in the Air Force prior to the start of the 1959 season, even his wild imagination could not have conceived the changes he was about to encounter. The Packers, the city, and the entire National Football League were on the cusp of never being the same again.

"That's how much Lombardi meant," Kramer said. "He came in and turned everything upside down. It happened fast. If you didn't get with the program, you were out of the program."

The first thing to be turned upside down was the Packers' administration office and not necessarily personnel. Upon his initial visit to Green Bay to sign his first contract, Lombardi was dismayed by the office's physical condition. He did not like what

---

[4]Izenberg, tape, *A Man Named Lombardi*.

the appearance connoted. There appeared to be as much disarray in the office as there had been on the field.

"He believed if you were going to be a successful professional organization, you had to look and act like a successful professional organization," Kramer said.

Lombardi ordered the facilities to be renovated. By the time he returned with his family to establish residency, a total makeover was almost complete. Peeling walls had been resurfaced and painted. Creaky floors had been repaired. New furniture had been purchased. A purge of old newspapers, magazines, and various other pieces of clutter had been completed with the order of never allowing such a mess to occur again.[5]

The message of the renovation transcended cosmetic appearance. The makeover of the Packers that was soon to take place on the field was a complete overhaul compared to the tune-up of the facilities.

Giving a facelift to an office is pretty simple stuff compared to replacing a spirit of complacency with one bursting from urgency for grabbing a championship edge.

"It was pretty loose around the club the year before Lombardi took over," tackle Bob Skoronski said. "We had heard he was pretty tough and would take no crap. He came in and made his mark on day one."

Lombardi imposed a standard of discipline so stringent it seemed the Packers could almost will their way to victory.

"On the first day he met with us, he talked about how important it was to be a professional on and off the field," Skoronski said. "I think striving to be a complete professional had as much to do with becoming a champion as anything else."[6]

In spite of the Packers' previous lackluster play, the cupboard wasn't bare of talent when Lombardi arrived. There was a solid nucleus of raw talent. It had simply slipped into a state of atrophy, desperately in need of revitalization.

"He inherited thirteen guys who either went on to the Hall of Fame or played in the Pro Bowl," said guard Jerry Kramer. "The talent was there. He just had to put it together."[7]

---

[5]Maraniss, *When Pride Still Mattered*, p. 206.
[6]Izenberg, tape, *A Man Named Lombardi*.
[7]Ibid.

This man was the Best

Paul Hornung

HOF 88

Ron Kramer learned about life from Coach Vince Lombardi and lived the fun part of it with teammate and best friend Paul Hornung.

Lombardi carefully purged players who did not fit into the system of his vision and relentlessly drove those who did to a conference crown in 1960.

The coach had tunnel vision. That vision left a lasting impression on his players the year center Jim Ringo showed up for contract negotiations accompanied by an agent. Lombardi preferred to negotiate directly with a player. Shortly after the meeting began,

Lombardi asked the two visitors to step outside his office so that he could make a call.

The coach called Skoronski, a starting tackle who resided year-round in Green Bay, and asked him to report immediately to the locker room.

"He had me make five or six snaps and said that was good enough," Skoronski said. "You're my center next year."[8]

Lombardi returned to his office to suggest Ringo's agent begin negotiations with Philadelphia. His client had just been traded to the Eagles.

Lombardi was not the tyrannical dictator some members of the media had painted him to be. He was possessed, however, by uncompromising commitment to the concept of the total team.

Guard Fuzzy Thurston considers it a privilege to have played for—and survived—the relentless coach.

"He was the most demanding man I ever met in my life," Thurston said. "He never took a step back from anyone. Don't get in his way because he'll beat you. If you didn't get with the program, you were gone. Simple as that."

McGee was often the target of Lombardi's uncompromising philosophy.

"He established a basic fear in all of his players" McGee said. "He made you afraid to make mental mistakes. You could mess up physically, but he wouldn't tolerate mental mistakes. We didn't make many because we were so disciplined. If a team beat us, they beat us. We didn't beat ourselves."

Lombardi had a gift for being able to squeeze two quarts of juice out of one orange. He did so by honing pure physical talent while reaching into the players' psyches. He created an aura of confidence that simply refused to tolerate defeat. If there was a will to accomplish something, they could certainly find a way.

He was fearless, tough, and demanding. Despite his idiosyncrasies, he was always fair. Certainly there were players who didn't particularly enjoy the techniques Lombardi believed in so passionately. But the respect he generated was universal and unshakable. No one questioned his character and ethics.

"The way he lived his life was a living example of leadership," said quarterback Bart Starr. "He was a rigidly practical person who

---

[8]Ibid.

had an established set of priorities and never wavered. It was God, family, and then the Packers. He never simply talked about doing things the right way ... he lived that way. That's the most noble form of leadership ... leading by example. He attended Mass at seven a.m. every day the entire nine years I was with him."

Starr still smiles at a memory of what Hall of Fame tackle Henry Jordan once said about Lombardi.

"Henry said: 'If you ever heard the way he would chew out our butts at practice, you'd know why he felt he had to go to Mass every day,'" Starr recalled.

The commitment Lombardi expected from his players was nothing short of the one he demanded of himself. His personal drive did not make things easy. It just made the team successful. Those players who survived did so as men.

"Before a game, he set a scene where he kind of took a football game off the field and applied it to family and personal existence," remarked Hall of Famer Willie Davis.

"He'd say 'I'd like for you to imagine that here's a group of guys that are coming into your home and are personally challenging you to a contest in front of family and friends. You're going to have to prove you are a man or you're going to have to live with it for the rest of your lives.'

"By the time we took that field, every Green Bay Packer felt he was not only playing to determine who was the best football team, but also to determine just how strong his manhood was."[9]

It was tough, but the players came to understand.

"He was a tough boss," said defensive back Willie Wood. "He was a hard guy to work for, but he had a real feel for players. He was always in your corner."

Lombardi's principle of equality toward each human being significantly impacted the social consciousness of the entire Green Bay community.

Green Bay was an almost exclusively white community at the time the Packers started their ascent to the top of the sporting world. So much so, in fact, that any strange young African-American male was immediately assumed to be a new Packer player.

Lombardi was possessed by a beautiful ignorance for any color other than the green and gold of the Green Bay Packers. All players

---

[9]Ibid.

and people with whom the coach had contact were treated with equal respect.

It was that same respect he expected to be practiced by each member of the team.

"If I ever hear 'nigger' or 'dago' or 'kike' or anything like that around here, regardless of who you are, you're through with me," Lombardi told his men. "You can't play for me if you have any kind of prejudice."[10]

Lombardi backed up his sentiment by becoming the first NFL coach to assign training camp roommates by alphabetical order without racial consideration.[11]

"I got to Green Bay in 1963," said former All Pro linebacker Dave Robinson. "It's difficult to understand the racial tensions that existed then compared to now. Lombardi simply wouldn't tolerate any type of prejudice."

Robinson also appreciates Kramer for his consideration.

"Ron made a teammate feel at ease," Robinson said. "He was the kind of guy that you could talk to about anything. I consider Ron one of my white brothers. We still call ourselves vanilla and chocolate."

In his own inimitable way, Lombardi also let it be known he expected the community to act in similar fashion regarding racial cohesion.

Through his unshakable principle, the African-American community of Green Bay experienced a measurable positive transition.

Although a free spirit away from the field, Kramer was the prototype of the player to most perfectly fit into the Lombardi mold. Physically, he was strong and quick. Mentally, he possessed a football instinct most often seen in quarterbacks.

Even more critical, however, were Kramer's work ethic and commitment to discipline.

"I had an early start," Kramer said. "Hell, my parents taught me discipline from the first time I can remember. Lombardi was tough, but so was my father. The thing about both of them was that they were fair. The discipline was wonderful. I loved it."

---

[10]Lombardi Jr., *What It Takes to Be #1*, pp. 86–87.
[11]Ibid., p. 87.

Lombardi's discipline and toughness emanated from the same source as Kramer's. He was the son of Italian immigrants who landed at Ellis Island in search of a better life than what was offered in the Old World.

His father was a butcher and demanded his children strive to make the most of the opportunity he sweat so hard to provide. After spending two years in the seminary studying to become a priest, Lombardi opted to study at Fordham University, where the seeds of his future were planted on the football field.

A starting guard on Fordham's legendary "Seven Rocks of Granite" offensive line, Lombardi developed a toughness that was relentless throughout the rest of his life.

That toughness bore a basic football philosophy. A game would take care of itself if a system was perfected in practice ... over and over and over again.

His practices went a few steps beyond demanding. They were brutal.

Even more impressive than his physical demands was the psychological mastery he practiced with the precision of a Swiss clock.

"Lombardi calculated every move he made," Kramer said. "He knew when to pat a guy on the back and when to leave a guy alone. He also knew when a good kick in the ass meant more than calling the right play. He was smarter than any other coach in the league. It wasn't even close."

Lombardi was smart enough to realize players win and lose games. Without physically talented athletes, Harry Houdini couldn't coach a team to a championship. Any coach who believes he can win the race without the horses is a bigger fool than the horses themselves.

Good coaches put their players in a position to succeed. Great coaches take it one step further. They instill into their players a will to win.

That was Vince Lombardi.

Could Lombardi have rewritten history without the talented players he assembled at Green Bay?

Probably not.

But could those same players have generated the degree of sustained success at Green Bay without Lombardi?

"Absolutely not!" claims Kramer.

"It all started with Lombardi," Kramer continued. "We had

talent, no doubt about it. But talent alone is nothing more than a beautiful lady sitting home alone on a Saturday night."

All the Packers were wise enough to realize if it was done Lombardi's way, victory was waiting at the end of the season.

There are many good field managers who make an excellent living as a head coach in the National Football League. They are adept at devising a thorough game plan and clever enough to make adjustments at the half.

Throughout history, though, only a handful have shaped minds and molded character in the Lombardi fashion.

For Kramer, the lessons learned are still lived today.

14 *The Habit of Winning*

Ron Kramer keeps a copy of the Vince Lombardi speech that did the most to shape Kramer's career, as well as the rest of his life. He's made copies and often gives them to friends to explain the legend for whom he was privileged to play.

THE HABIT OF WINNING

Winning is not a sometime thing. You don't win once-in-a-while. You don't do things right once-in-a-while. You do them right all the time. Winning is a habit. Unfortunately, so is losing. There is no room for second place. There is only one place in my game and that is first place. I have finished second twice in my time at Green Bay and I don't ever want to finish second again. It is and always has been an American zeal to be first in anything we do. The object—to win!

Every time a football player goes out to play, he's got to play from the ground up. From the soles of his feet right up to his head. Every inch of him has to play. Some guys play with their heads. That's OK—you've got to be smart to be number one in any business, but in football, you've got to play with your heart. With every fiber of your body. If you are lucky enough to find a guy with a lot of head and a lot of heart, he's never going to come off the field second.

Running a football team is no different from running any other kind of organization—an Army, a political party, a business. The problems are the same. The objective is to win. To beat the other guy. Maybe that sounds hard or cruel. I don't think it is.

It is a reality of life that men are competitive and the most competitive games draw the most competitive men. That's why they're there—to compete. They know the rules and the objectives when they get in the game. The objective is to win—fairly, squarely, decently, by the rules—but to win. And in truth, I have never known a man worth his salt who in the long run, deep down in his heart, did not appreciate the grind—the discipline. There is something in good men that really yearns for, needs ... discipline and the harsh reality of head-to-head combat.

I don't say these things because I believe in the "brute" nature of man or that man must be brutalized to be combative. I believe in God and I believe in human decency. But I firmly believe that any man's finest hour, his greatest fulfillment to all he holds dear, is the moment when he has worked his heart out in a good cause and lies exhausted on the field of battle victorious.

It was considered Lombardi's credo—his greatest gift to Green Bay and his men.

"Until he came to Green Bay, the Packers didn't know how to win," Kramer said. "We had talent, but there's a difference between having ability and knowing how to win. He didn't coach just football. He showed us how the underlying principles of the game can be applied to life. He taught us that winning demands discipline and character. It's the same thing for every walk of life."

Kramer could readily identify with the character of Lombardi. The coach came from an immigrant Italian family in Brooklyn, New York. Lombardi learned to embrace the same type of family discipline as Kramer had.

Lombardi never had the physical tools Kramer possessed. He was squat and undersized. Nevertheless, he drove himself to become one of the rocks on Fordham University's legendary "Seven Rocks of Granite" offensive line.

One of his coaching stops along his path to Green Bay was as an assistant to Red Blaik at the United States Military Academy. It was there that he served as an intermediary between Blaik and General Douglas MacArthur. The two were close friends and MacArthur was a passionate fan of the Army football team. Lombardi was often instructed by Blaik to keep the general informed about the condition of the cadets from West Point.

Lombardi's position was one that oozed with discipline. It also was a situation in which he felt comfortably at home.

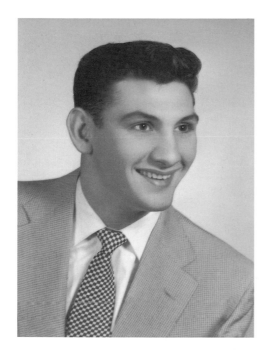

Even without the cap and gown, Ron looked ready to attend the University of Michigan after graduating from East Detroit High, where he left standards that still haven't been matched in the state of Michigan.

With a mug like that, who wants to cover it with a face mask? That's the way Kramer played at Michigan and loved every moment. (Reproduced by permission from Bentley Historical Library, University of Michigan)

College Football Hall of Famers Howard "Hop-a-Long" Cassady (left) and Ron Kramer go head-to-head in the traditional Ohio State–Michigan showdown. Kramer must be tough, playing without a face mask.

A slightly different look at the starting offense of the 1961 Green Bay championship team that was considerably different and better than any football team on the planet.

Ron was home in Detroit, but proud to be a Packer in the traditional Thanksgiving Day game against the Lions.

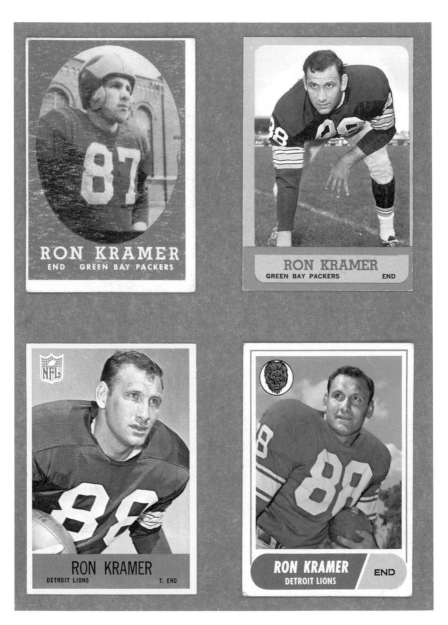

When he was a kid, Ron never dreamed he would be featured on bubble gum cards.

Check out the outfits on this
dazzling duo as Ron Kramer
(*right*) teams with the late J. P.
McCarthy (celebrated radio
talk host) to raise money for
charity.

Ron never missed an opportunity to share time with his
University of Michigan coach Bennie Oosterbaan.

After being elected to the College Football Hall of Fame in 1978, Ron Kramer was honored during halftime at a University of Michigan Football game.

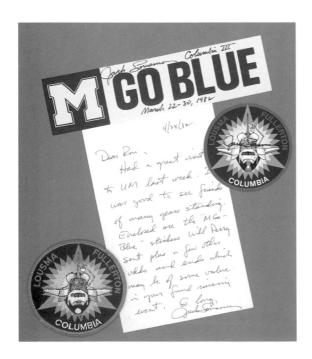

Former Michigan teammate and astronaut Jack Lousma took this "M Go Blue" sticker to the moon and signed it to his friend Ron.

A beautiful 50th birthday for Ron, with mom Adeline holding a cover of *Sports Illustrated* featuring her son and Tom Maentz.

Ron Kramer and Marie Lombardi at the 1975 event where Vince Lombardi, Ron Kramer, and eight other players were inducted into the Green Bay Packers Hall of Fame.

Not everyone can get a golf tip from President Gerald Ford. Of course, Ron Kramer is not quite like everyone else.

In 1995, Ron Kramer served as an honorary Green Bay Packer captain and was surrounded by captains (*left to right*) Jeff Thomason, Dorsey Levens, and Gilbert Brown.

Ron Kramer was one proud papa when he served as an honorary captain for the Detroit Lions with daughter Cassie and son Kurt in attendance.

Two Michigan legends—Bo Schembechler and Ron Kramer—during halftime at the Big House.

Daughter Cassie was proud to join Ron when he served as honorary captain for a game in Green Bay in 2001. Check out Kramer's rookie picture from 1957 in the corner.

Paul Hornung always said: "To get to me, you have to go through Kramer." Well, it looks like Kramer's lady friend Barbara Giorgio did just that.

The aura of Coach Vince Lombardi still burns brightly inside of Ron Kramer's heart. Kramer and Barbara Giorgio stand beneath the bigger-than-life statue of the coach in front of Lambeau Field.

University of Michigan stalwarts (*left to right*): broadcasters Steve Courtney and Frank Beckmann, Ron Kramer, and former Michigan tackle and current Wolverine broadcaster Jim Brandstatter.

Three University of Michigan legends (*left to right*): Ron Kramer, Don Canham, and Al Wistert.

Were there three better than these former tight ends? Sharing old stories are (*left to right*) Ron Kramer, Jackie Smith, and Mike Ditka.

Maybe a little too old to spin around on the dance floor, but Ron Kramer shows his old basketball buddy Bob Vander Werf he can still balance objects on his head.

Filled with irreplaceable memorabilia, Kramer describes the interior of his home as a "little cluttered."

The University of Michigan football jersey that Kramer wore in his last game is framed under glass and hangs above the fireplace. Kramer's number 87 was retired after his final game.

There's plenty to smile about. Dr. David Dobies, the Genysys Hospital heart specialist, saved Ron Kramer's life after Kramer suffered a heart attack in early 2007.

"West Point taught me discipline, regularity," Lombardi said. "Red Blaik taught me the meaning of organization. And Green Bay taught me to be successful."[12]

Long before he arrived at West Point, Lombardi learned to refuse the concept of being a good loser. Representing the United States Army, the cadets were conditioned always to conduct themselves as men. Nevertheless, it was impossible not to feel the fire of their assistant coach.

"Lombardi had a theory about losing," Kramer smiled. "He said let the other teams learn how to become good losers. He wanted no part of it."

Many coaches mimic the words about knowing how to win. Lombardi had the wisdom, strength, character, and will to put them into action. Most importantly, he had a gift for imparting those same principles into his men.

There was nothing complex about the essence of his program. Its strength, in fact, lay in the simplicity of its foundation.

- DISCIPLINE   "Work and sacrifice, perseverance, competitive drive, selflessness, and respect for authority are the price that each one must pay to achieve any goal that is worthwhile."[13]
- REPETITION   "You don't do what is right once in a while, but all the time."[14]
- CHARACTER   "The great hope of society is the individual character. If you would create something, you must be something."[15]
- TEAMWORK   "I've been in football all my life, gentlemen, and I don't know whether I'm particularly qualified to be a part of anything else, except I consider it a great game, a game of many assets, by the way, and I think a symbol of what this country's best attributes are: courage and stamina and a coordinated efficiency or teamwork."[16] Lombardi's approach to the mechanical aspects of the game was simple—blocking and tackling. Those that do

---

[12]Lombardi, Jr., *What It Takes to Be #1*, p. 73.
[13]Ibid., p. 95.
[14]Ibid., p. 251.
[15]Ibid., p. 71.
[16]Ibid., p. 15.

them best win. Those that do them with a lesser degree of efficiency lose. Simple as that.

"There was nothing complex about his system," Kramer said. "It simply demanded commitment. He got himself involved with everything. He stressed discipline, repetition, character, and teamwork. We had to work our asses off, but there was never any question about what he wanted to accomplish and what was expected of everybody."

What was most expected by Lombardi was commitment to total effort.

"I'd rather have a player with 50 percent ability and 100 percent desire because the guy with 100 percent desire is going to play every day, so you can make a system to fit what he can do," Lombardi said. "The other guy—the guy with 100 percent ability and 50 percent desire—can screw up your whole system because one day he'll be out there waltzing around."[17]

Lombardi's system included a series of drills designed to develop those qualities of the complete person in which he so fervently believed. They ranged from the sadistically physical to the gentle sublime.

There was "the nutcracker" drill in which receivers and linebackers brutally pounded each other all week in practice in preparation for what was sure to be a much more serene game day on Sunday.

There was a hand clapping exercise in which each player learned to clap in unison with the rest of the team.

"Lombardi would get all the players on offense together," Kramer explained. "He'd tell us that on the count of two, he wanted all of us to clap. The first time we did it, I wondered what the hell was going on. Then he shouted the count: 'Ready ... hut, hut.' We all had to clap. We were supposed to clap our hands so that everyone was doing it at precisely the same time.

"When the drill started, we sounded like a garage band completely out of tune. There would be clap, clap from one group of guys and then clap, clap, clap from another. He wouldn't let us stop till we got it down to one single clap."

---

[17]Ibid., p. 109.

The subtle drill was designed to create a sense of teamwork. After a few days of practice, the result was ear-hammeringly apparent. The single voluminous clap sounded as crisp as the clashing cymbals of the University of Michigan Marching Band.

Another drill designed to create teamwork involved the blocking sled. Lombardi's eyes would start to gleam at the sight of the old football practice device.

"He loved standing on the back of that sled while we hit it," Kramer recalled. "He'd stand there like Alfred Hitchcock directing a movie. He'd call out: 'Hut … hut … hut.' Then we had to hit the pads at the same time. He could tell if one shoulder was off by a hundredth of a second. We'd go over it and over it and over it till we got it perfect. Then we'd do it some more. The harder we hit, the more he loved it. He would yell: 'I can feel it … I can feel it.'

"When he finally thought we had had enough, he'd give that little cackle of his and say: 'Alright, gentlemen … we'll start over again tomorrow.'"

And, of course, there was the running of the "sweep." After each practice, Lombardi had the offense running the sweep against the defense until he finally got tired or the sun had set and there was nothing more to see.

"He believed in repetition," Kramer said. "He always said there's a habit of winning and a habit of losing and you can fall into either one. He also said: 'You are NOT going to get in the habit of losing as long as I'm here.'"

When Sundays came, the Packers were prepared. It then became a matter of execution and Lombardi allowed his players to perform what they had practiced all week. While he was stunningly inspirational simply pacing the sidelines, he allowed quarterback Bart Starr the freedom to call his own plays.

"That's true because Coach Lombardi had us so well prepared we knew what to do," Starr confirmed. "He was such an outstanding leader and teacher that we actually loved to go to practices and meetings."

While the portrait of Lombardi is sometimes painted as being tyrannical, those closest to him appreciated his sense of humor.

"He was dynamic and explosive, but most people didn't see the other side of him," Starr said. "He loved to laugh. That's a tremendous quality in any person. He had a great sense of humor. He could cry just as easily and was a very sensitive person. He was very tough, but very fair."

Most players appreciated Lombardi's sense of humor. Kramer rarely missed an opportunity to exchange barbs with the coach at precisely the right moment.

Preparing for one game at Cleveland, Lombardi cautioned his players about the possible dangers of playing in front of eighty thousand people in old Municipal Stadium.

"What's the big deal, Vince?" Kramer lightened the serious team meeting. "I was used to playing before one hundred thousand back at Michigan."

Wide receiver Max McGee rarely missed an opportunity to insert a smile into the intensity of the Packers' practices. Before the start of each training camp, Lombardi reviewed the fundamentals of the game that haven't changed since foot first met the ball.

"This is a football," Lombardi would bark while holding a pigskin before a meeting of his men.

"Slow down, Coach," McGee cracked, "you're going a little too fast."

And Lombardi never missed an opportunity to jab his players when the occasion arose.

Because of chronic back problems, Kramer was allowed to lie on the floor in front of Lombardi when the team was reviewing game film. Before one meeting McGee decided to join Kramer in the more comfortable position.

Lombardi looked down at his mischievous wide receiver and barked: "Get your ass out of there McGee. I've already got one bear rug, I don't need two."

Kramer appreciated the opportunity to communicate with the coach. He believes it demonstrated the confidence Lombardi carried.

"When a man is confident in himself, he's not afraid to be challenged," Kramer said. "The guys who had the most fun with him were Hornung and me. He would make sly remarks to us and we would give it right back. He loved people who would do that. You could argue your point, but if you were wrong, that was the end of it."

Lombardi also was open to suggestions about plays.

"He always said that we knew our positions better than he did," Kramer said. "He said that all of his work was experimental. He merely drew up the plays. We were the guys who put them into practice. That's the sign of an intelligent man."

Often Lombardi would act on the suggestion of his players to refine a play he had designed.

"Intellectually, he totally outclassed every coach in the league," Kramer said.

Kramer remembers watching game film with the rest of the team when Lombardi criticized a block Kramer made and re-ran it about a dozen times.

"Vinnie, if you can do it better, why don't you go out there and knock that big son of a bitch on his ass?" Kramer cracked.

Lombardi appreciated Kramer's confidence. His oversized nostrils would begin to ruffle before he broke into a laugh.

"Ron was the only player that called him Vinnie," Boyd Dowler said. "Ron would say stuff like: 'Come on, Vinnie … settle down.' Lombardi would shake his head, look the other way, and smile."

Kramer also had a gift for infusing the right touch of humor into a situation to push his teammates over the edge.

"Lombardi used to get on [guard] Jerry Kramer all the time during practice," Dowler recalled. "He used to yell at Jerry: 'You're not coming off the ball quick enough … you're not coming off the ball quick enough.'

"If we had trouble getting started in a game, Ron would come back into the huddle and slap Jerry on the helmet. 'You're just not coming off the ball quick enough,' Ron would crack. That was always good for a laugh and usually got us going."

The banter, the head banging, the grunts and the groans all were designed to create a sense of unselfishness. With any Lombardi-led team, no single player was bigger than the sum of all. Teamwork, not individuals, will always dictate the course of a grueling season.

Sometimes, of course, teamwork is demonstrated in the strangest ways.

The Packers were staying in Palo Alto in preparation for a Sunday game against the 49ers. On Tuesday evening, a few of the boys were bored and couldn't resist the bright lights of San Francisco, a short drive away. After the 11 p.m. bed check, Kramer and five cohorts slipped out the back door to help support the entertainment segment of San Francisco's economy.

Linebacker Dan Currie decided to challenge Fuzzy Thurston to an Olympic drinking contest. Thurston, the NFL's unofficial champion, was never one to refuse a challenge.

The two went toe-to-toe and glass-to-glass until Currie finally passed out. Thurston celebrated his victory by doing a set of push-ups on the piano.

Being responsible teammates, the players got a pitcher full of ice to revive their fallen linebacker. All seemed fine when they returned to their rooms at around 5 a.m. and then reported to practice on time.

Before the workout, Lombardi singled out Thurston who wasn't in his room when it was checked.

"I want all you guys to watch what's going to happen to Fuzzy," Lombardi addressed the team. "He's going to be doing some extra wind sprints for me today."

Kramer slyly looked at each of his fellow miscreants.

"We all knew what was going through Fuzzy's mind," Kramer laughed. "He's thinking—what about the other five assholes that went with me?"

At the precise moment—almost as if it had been rehearsed—Fuzzy's cohorts raised their arms and took a step forward to admit they had accompanied Fuzzy on his San Francisco escapade. Without saying a word, all five joined Fuzzy in the wind sprints.

"Lombardi loved it," Kramer said. "You could just feel him thinking—that's my team ... this is really a team."

The incident wasn't exactly a part of the Packers' playbook, but it emphasized to all the brotherhood of the Packers.

"We worked together ... we did things together ... and we took the heat together," Kramer remembers with pride. "That was all a testament to Lombardi. It all goes back to him."

15 *Is That Tough Enough?*

Richard Afflis was an unheralded journeyman lineman who played in anonymity for the Green Bay Packers from 1950 through 1954 when he decided to make a career change.

Although content with his job in the NFL, at the suggestion of Leo Nomellini, Afflis decided to take a shot at professional wrestling. Nomellini was a defensive lineman for the San Francisco 49ers who wrestled professionally during the off-seasons. He pegged his friend as a natural for the sport.

The timing was perfect for Afflis. The Indianapolis native capitalized on the growing TV popularity of the sport that probably he didn't even imagine. He created a character called Dick the Bruiser and proclaimed himself "The World's Most Dangerous Wrestler."

Late-night talk show giant David Letterman—also an Indianapolis native—named his CBS Letterman Show house band "The World's Most Dangerous Band" as a tribute to The Bruiser.

Dick the Bruiser quickly rose to cult figure status and Afflis roared as his income skyrocketed past what he earned from the Packers for bashing heads on Sundays while wearing a Green Bay helmet.

Afflis developed his Dick the Bruiser character into a sadistic executioner who thrived on pain—both delivered and received. He was a beer-guzzling, raspy-voiced, uncontrollable madman whose zany antics always left loyal TV viewers wondering what to expect from him the following week.

Not so ironically, Afflis sometimes allowed the theatrics of the ring to transcend into daily life. He wound up in several celebrated genuine head-stomping, eye-gouging, and body-slamming scuffles in the real world.

It came as no surprise to Dick the Bruiser's former teammates who had grown accustomed to the bizarre always surrounding the former Richard Afflis.

"He was a little different," understated Gary Knafelc whose first year with the Packers was The Bruiser's last.

Knafelc remembers when Afflis exploded into a rampage after undergoing a root canal. He vowed never to undergo the procedure again. To prove his commitment to any dentist who doubted his resolve, Afflis had all his teeth extracted.

Another incident arose in 1954 when the Packers were traveling by train to California to play the San Francisco 49ers and Los Angeles Rams on the last two Sundays of the season. The trip, in those days, took three days. Players would pass time playing cards and drinking beer.

A contest to determine the toughest man on the train emerged between Afflis and mammoth defensive tackle Jerry Helluin.

Afflis first guzzled a beer before crushing the empty can on his forehead. Helluin did the same. Afflis then downed another beer before placing the can at the bend of his elbow and crushing it with his bicep. Helluin did the same. Afflis quickly inhaled another beer and set the can on his throat and crushed it between his chin and chest. Helluin did the same.

Finally, Afflis washed down the first three beers with a fourth and crushed the empty can on the bridge of his nose that caused a river of blood to run down his face.

Helluin stared at his radically eccentric teammate and simply shook his head.

"You win," Helluin told the future Bruiser.

"Afflis was a strange character who got no greater satisfaction in life than leveling a defender," Knafelc said. "You couldn't hurt him, but he could sure do some damage to you."

Knafelc certainly doesn't equate Afflis—or his Dick the Bruiser character—to Ron Kramer. But he is convinced both players derived intense gratification from delivering a bone-crunching blow to any defender who had the misguided tenacity to stand in their way.

"Ron was a clean player," Knafelc said. "He didn't have to play dirty. But when he wanted to be nasty, he could be third-degree nasty. He enjoyed the contact. Giving or taking it didn't matter. He never did any of that taunting or trash talking that you see in today's game. He simply leveled a player and walked back to the huddle to get ready for the next play."

Knafelc remembers one particular practice when linebacker Dan Currie jumped the count and knocked Kramer on that part of the body that is generally used to sit upon.

Kramer got up without saying a word. On the next play, and without jumping the count, Kramer delivered a wallop on Currie that sent him flying five yards backward before he finally landed back on earth. Again, Kramer never said a word. He simply turned around and walked back to the huddle to prepare for the next play.

"Of all the guys who could have been a dink, Ron never was," Knafelc said. "He never talked down to anyone or never tried to make another player look bad. He knew how good he was. He didn't have to flaunt it."

Before he played football for the University of Colorado, Knafelc had run into his share of supposed "tough guys." His father owned a saloon that became a favorite hangout for cowboys and roustabouts. There were enough scuffles in the bar to fill a full slate of Friday night wrestling.

"I had seen my share of fights," Knafelc said. "You didn't have to worry about the loud mouths who popped off about everything. The one you had to worry about was the quiet guy minding his own business in the corner. Don't get him mad or you might get more trouble than you can handle."

Knafelc would have bet on Kramer against any cowboy or roustabout foolish enough to dare him into a scuffle.

"Ron was one of the strongest guys I ever met," Knafelc said. "I would have rather fought [Ray] Nitschke than Kramer any day. You ask any defensive back we played. Of all the guys they covered, the one they least wanted to try to bring down was Kramer."

Knafelc particularly remembers one game against Cleveland.

"I swear Ron played the whole game without ever being knocked off his feet," Knafelc marveled. "He used to drag tacklers down the field like they were riding a train."

Opposing teams only had to see Nitschke on Sundays. The Packers' offense had to run against him every day in practice from the first day of training camp through the end of the season.

"That was a big part of the reason for our success," Kramer said. "We had the best offense in the league running against the best defense every day. Everybody had to know all the plays. And everybody had to hit and make plays in practice to stay in the lineup."

Nitschke was an assassin at middle linebacker with no regard for the body he was pursuing or his own. With his steely eyes and missing front teeth, he was a haunting figure that looked like a de-fanged vampire.

"The nutcracker" was a drill that Vince Lombardi loved to run before the start of practice. He had the wide receivers and tight ends going one-on-one against the linebackers with no holds barred. The last man standing was champion for a day.

The hitting was fierce, far more devastating than what they would have to endure on Sundays. Lombardi appreciated the violence of the game. He believed that to survive, a player needed character and had to be prepared. The "nutcracker" separated the men from the boys.

Most players abhorred the drill. Kramer loved it.

"Nitschke and I would go nose to nose," Kramer said. "Pop! Bam! Pow! We'd be snarling and hitting each other. The whistle would blow and we'd still be beating the hell out of each other."

On game days, Nitschke transformed into a character that seemed to be visiting from some other world.

"I was the only guy that would go close to him before a game," Kramer said. "When he wanted to warm up, he'd start hitting you. He hit people so hard, no one wanted to get near him. I loved it. We used to beat on each other. It made playing the game a whole lot easier."

Dave Robinson was another linebacker that Kramer enjoyed tangling with in the nutcracker.

"Ron loved to hit," Robinson said. "So did I. We both drove into each other trying to make the pads go 'POP.' Lombardi could tell just by the sound how hard his guys were hitting. If you made a good hit, he wouldn't say anything but 'Wow.' That's what we wanted to hear. We wanted to hear that 'Wow.'"

While Kramer thrived on the sadistic intensity of the nutcracker drill, the rest of the Packers merely learned how to survive it.

"I tried to get in line first to get it over with," Knafelc said. "I tried to get my head into Nitschke's chest and turn him a little so that I could neutralize his fist. He used to wait for you with his fist clenched so he could bust you. When he got done with one guy, he'd look up and growl, 'NEXT!'"

At least one player devised a more cunning scheme so as not to have to take on the resident maniacal middle linebacker at all.

Max McGee was one of the most gifted receivers in the league.

He was born with glue on his hands and made acrobatic catches look as easy as picking popcorn out of a paper bag.

McGee simply did not like contact. He didn't enjoy hitting people. And as sure as Green Bay January snow, he did not like to get hit.

"Max devised a system for getting in line and somehow slipping to the back when it was his turn to run the drill," Knafelc said. "I watched two years of film on him and I swear he never appeared once in the nutcracker."

McGee never denied his distaste for physical contact.

"Max didn't block," Kramer said. "He couldn't block. Every time he got hit in the head he was dizzy for two days. I remember one game playing against Los Angeles. The play was going the other way and one of the linebackers hit him.

"He came back to the huddle and said to me: 'Did you see what that big ol' linebacker did to me? That bastard hit me in the head and I'm going whacko.'"

Kramer simply smiled.

"I told him to relax," Kramer said. "I'll take care of things. On the next play I blindsided the son of a bitch. I really leveled him. I went back to the huddle and told Max he didn't have to worry any more."

In 1958, McGee and Billy Howton bet one hundred dollars on who would make the most blocks during the season. McGee made two … and won the wager.

Kramer relished the essence of physical contact and appreciated throwing a crisp, chilling block as much as he did catching a pass for a first down.

"Contact is hard to understand for people who never played the sport," Kramer explained. "You know you are going to take some hits. I respected a good clean hit on me. You have to. That's what the game is about. To defeat the man you're playing, you have to block.

"Physical contact is the makeup of the human male. If you examine football, it's just like war. There are guys in the trenches. Sometimes you throw a bomb. You try to gain ground. It encompasses every element of the military. There's an aerial attack and a ground attack. If it rains hard enough, you have to go to your naval attack."

Blocking isn't the snazzy paint and sparkling chrome of a new car. It's the pistons and crankshaft that are rarely seen and never mind if they get sprayed with a little oil.

Even the best blocks don't show up in game statistics. There's nothing prettier, though, to the players on the field.

"I wasn't the only player on the field that could block," Kramer said. "Everybody blocked … except for McGee who absolutely hated it and just couldn't do it. If you look at the old films, you'll notice Bart Starr usually left the field with a clean uniform. We rarely let the quarterback get touched."

Kramer still takes considerable pride in the fact that the blocking of the whole meant just as much as the scoring by the few for the team to be successful.

"When Paul Hornung or Jim Taylor took a sweep into the end zone, that touchdown didn't belong simply to them," Kramer said. "When Bart Starr threw a touchdown pass to me, it didn't belong only to us.

"The touchdowns belonged as much to Fuzzy Thurston or Forrest Gregg or Jerry Kramer or Bob Skoronski or Jim Ringo or Norm Masters or anybody who completed their assignment and took a defender out of the play. It all had to work together. If one assignment broke down, the whole play broke down. You score touchdowns as a team. That's the way Lombardi coached us. If you don't block, you don't score. Simple as that."

No one at his particular position consistently blocked with the proficiency of Kramer at his.

From game observations and studying film, Lombardi and the other coaches rated players weekly on blocking proficiency. Tight ends were expected to block at sixty-five percent on runs and eighty percent on pass plays. Kramer regularly checked in above eighty percent in both categories.

At a team meeting each week, Lombardi distributed rewards of twenty dollars to those players who excelled at their assignments in a variety of categories. Kramer was a regular recipient. For the fourteen game regular season, Kramer would win twelve blocking awards.

"He would call us up to the front of the room and hand us the money," Kramer said. "The money didn't matter. It was an honor to be rewarded by him in front of your peers."

He paused a moment and then smiled.

"The extra twenty did help for a couple of rounds of cold after-practice refreshments," he said.

It didn't matter to Kramer whether the assignment called to block a linebacker or a maniacal, oversized defensive end.

"I loved hitting those guys," Kramer said. "First of all, he isn't sure if a pass is coming or if we're going to run the ball. He's got to be a little cautious. I'm not going to let him come in and just play around. That was my forte—intimidation. But not with my mouth. There's only one form of intimidation that's important. That's through your actions."

Efficient blocking often unfolds without being noticed by fans sitting in the stands. Most fans keep their eyes peeled to the running back or maybe the quarterback throwing the ball downfield. Some blocks, however, stand out like a pimple on the tip of Paris Hilton's nose.

Years ago while watching the game film against the Los Angeles Rams, even Kramer was impressed by one of his more memorable hits. Kramer not only hit Deacon Jones, he drove him into Lamar Lundy, the other defensive end on the opposite side of the field.

"I remember that one," he smiled. "I told Jones: 'Mr. Jones, I want you to meet Mr. Lundy.'"

Kramer never hit a player simply for the sake of getting in a cheap lick. Every block was delivered by design. And every one was sent with a message.

"I enjoyed the contact," Kramer said. "But I enjoyed all the other parts of the game, too. To be a complete player, you had to master everything. To be a winning team, everyone had to do his job."

That's the way Kramer and the Packers played. Contact was essential to make everything else unfold. Kramer loved it—during the games and all week long during practice.

Ray Nitschke could attest to that.

16 Lombardi's 12th Man

Ron Kramer's list of honors and achievements has to be considered impressive. It runs miles longer than the rap sheets on some of today's more flamboyant players.

He was a two-time football All-American at the University of Michigan where his jersey number 87 is retired. He is a member of the College Football Hall of Fame. He played on two NFL championship teams and was selected to a Pro Bowl. Some peers and experts claim he was the best tight end ever to play the game.

Humbly, Kramer appreciates the accolades.

None, however, compare to the compliment given by the patron saint of all NFL coaches.

Kramer was accorded that distinction when Green Bay legend Vince Lombardi acknowledged his all-around athleticism by calling him his "twelfth man on the field."

Those are heavy duty words from the mouth of any coach. Coming from Lombardi, they are the imprimatur, packing more wallop than a Papal blessing.

"It's touching," said Kramer, whose admiration of his former coach also borders on the spiritual.

"It's the nicest thing he could say about me. It still makes me feel good just thinking about it."

Lombardi didn't invent the tight end position. He did, however, recognize its untapped potential. He believed the position had been woefully underutilized and was the key to the success of his awesome Green Bay sweep.

To realize the position he had imagined, however, necessitated a singular type of athlete. At the time, that player had yet to be molded and finally defined.

Practice time was brutal at Green Bay, but Ron Kramer found one moment to stretch out.

The prototype had to block like a tackle, run like a safety, snag passes like a wide receiver, and think like a quarterback. And one final ingredient—he needed the savage disposition of the most mediaeval linebacker.

The tight end Lombardi envisioned needed the agility to level a defender with an impossible block and the fearlessness to ignore the vicious hits his own body would certainly sustain from the position.

A player like that had yet to be found.

Then along came Kramer.

Kramer possessed all the physical assets required to play the position as Lombardi envisioned it. He also had the intangibles that allowed his physical talent to put creases on the forehead of every opposing coach.

"That was the beauty of Ron," said Hall of Famer Paul Hornung. "The defense had to worry about trying to take him out of setting up the sweep and, at the same time, prevent him from taking a pass down the field. If he got his hands on the ball, it was a catch. And for a big SOB, he could run."

Kramer was wise enough to understand that the inherent nature of football is to accept physical pain—both inflicted and received. He was fearless with his body, yet disciplined enough to realize each play had to be executed precisely within a scheme, without reckless abandon.

Playing for Lombardi demanded complete commitment to

the concept of teamwork. No position was more important than another. If one assignment cracked, an entire play broke down. Even the slightest blemish of a single color changes the face of a rainbow into meaningless streaks in the sky.

"He called me his twelfth man because I could single block anybody," Kramer explained. "If you had a tight end who couldn't handle a defensive end or a linebacker on a single block, that means you had to use a double team block. A tight end who could single block allowed him to run the sweep the way he had dreamed it would work."

Forrest Gregg, the Hall of Fame tackle who lined up next to Kramer, got an up-close appreciation for his presence.

Gregg used to tell opponents before the first play of the game: "Don't worry about me … worry about that big SOB outside of you. He can be nasty."

Tight end—especially when Kramer played—is not the glamour position of flanker or wide receiver. Those are the "pretty boys" of the modern game. Some dance in the end zone after taking a pass all the way. They are marketing savvy. They are aware of every television camera angle and know just when and where to pose for optimum exposure.

"Tight end," Kramer explained, "is catching and blocking. Neither one is more important than the other. It's a transitional position. A lot of guys when playing the right side, all of a sudden screw things up when they move to the left.

"You have to keep everything in perspective as far as blocking situations occur. Every time the defense changes the scheme from odd to even or switches from a four-three, to a five-two or a three-man front, the blocking changes. You have to remember if you're on the right or left side. At the same time, you have to run the right pass pattern."

It sounds more complicated than a geometric theorem. Kramer concedes with a smile that his degree in psychology may actually have contributed a smidgen to his success on the field.

"A lot of people think the tight end isn't doing anything," Kramer continued. "If you're running a passing game, everybody's important because every man is assigned to handle a defender. No one can get released or the play breaks down.

"If I cleared an area out for Boyd Dowler or Max McGee and worked hard to keep it clear and one of them catches a pass, then it's my pass, too. That's the way we worked. We didn't care who threw the pass or who caught it. All that mattered was that we got it over the goal line. That's one reason we remain such close friends today. That was the genius of Lombardi."

Gary Knafelc enjoyed a unique perspective for watching the development of the man who would replace him.

"Two years ahead of him and two years behind," is the way Knafelc labels his Green Bay tenure with Kramer.

For two years while Kramer struggled to recuperate from knee surgery and re-establish the confidence that had once been as natural as green on the playing field, Knafelc was the starting tight end.

The problem was that he was playing out of position. He was a tugboat trying to knock out a freighter.

"I was really a wide receiver," Knafelc smiled at the memory. "I was 215 pounds trying to take out a linebacker or defensive end. I had to double up my blocking with Forrest Gregg and that left another defender open."

Along came Kramer at 250 pounds with an attitude of a recently neutered bull. Knafelc spent his last two years watching what he is convinced was the finest tight end to play the position.

"He was strong as steel with a nasty attitude," Knafelc said. "He was raw power. When he wanted to be nasty, he could be nasty. All within the rules, but he could be nasty. He just loved blocking. I hated it."

Knafelc understood the necessity of Kramer being groomed to take his position.

"That was the genius of Lombardi," Kramer explained. "It was all team with him. What was best for the team was best for everyone. It's hard to explain, but we were more than a team. We were like family—still are today."

Kramer did the same for his replacement when he decided he would have to leave the Packers for family reasons. Marv Fleming joined the Packers in 1963 and played through 1969. Like Kramer, Fleming was a ferocious blocker who also could catch passes.

"When I was thinking about leaving, I told Vince I would teach Marv everything I knew," Kramer said. "I think he learned his lessons pretty well."

It wasn't merely Kramer's brute force that makes Knafelc still marvel today. He still wonders how a player so big and so strong could be so quick, with the hands of a pianist.

"You judge a receiver by how many third down passes he catches," Knafelc said. "I'm not talking third and three or third and five. I'm talking third and eighteen or third and twenty. Ron made those catches like picking an apple from a tree. He never dropped a pass. Once his fingers touched, the ball was his.

"Ask any defensive back from that period who they least liked to cover. They'll all tell you it was Kramer. If he wasn't knocking someone over with a block, he was catching a pass. And once he did, that defender was going to pay a price for trying to take him down."

There's no question in Hornung's mind about how history should view Kramer.

"Ron Kramer and Mike Ditka were the two finest tight ends ever to play the game," he said.

Besides his willingness to block and his uncanny knack for holding on to passes, there was something special about Kramer that struck Knafelc from the first time they met.

"No question in my mind," Knafelc said. "He was the best pure athlete I have ever known. He could do everything. And he made it look so natural. If he were playing today, he could have been one of those players who didn't practice all week. He could come out on Sunday and still never miss a beat."

Of course, that wasn't done in the days when players had to work the off-seasons just to pay the bills on time. Knafelc, for instance, played the entire 1959 season with a broken left hand. He had it taped tightly before each game and practice. He sought treatment from a private doctor because he didn't want the Packers to know the severity of the injury.

"Coach Lombardi didn't like players who got hurt," he said. "Once you took yourself out of the lineup, there was a chance you'd never return."

Knafelc remains convinced about another couple of Kramer observations.

"Ron was a Hall of Fame player," he said with conviction. "He just didn't have the chance to play long enough. Ask anyone who played with him or against him. All the guys loved him. I know I want him on my side in any situation. I don't want to look across and see him on the other side of the ball."

Knafelc certainly got a good look at Kramer once he moved up to the position Knafelc held.

"I'm proud to tell people I kept the best tight end on the bench for two years," Knafelc cracked. "And then I had the privilege of watching him play for two years."

Given the opportunity, could Kramer have played in today's game?

"He could play today on any team," Knafelc is convinced. "The position belongs to him. The man has no fear."

Fear was never an option on any team Lombardi led. Especially not from his twelfth man.

17 *Hornung and Kramer*

After the Green Bay Packers humiliated the New York Giants, 37–0, in the 1961 NFL championship game, Paul Hornung sat in front of his locker and told a horde of writers and broadcasters from around the country about his friendship with Ron Kramer.

"If you want to get to me, you have to go through Ron Kramer," Hornung said.

Hornung stressed the relationship was the same on and off the field.

On that historic Sunday, Kramer had been particularly protective of his best buddy. The mammoth tight end exhibited a punishing display of blocking to help slice holes in the Giants' line that Old Mother Hubbard could have skipped through.

Hornung didn't miss any of them. He hit every one with speed and precision to score an NFL championship game record nineteen points. For the performance, he was voted the game's Most Valuable Player, earning a sparkling new Corvette.

"If the writers had known anything about football, they would have voted for Kramer," Hornung said.

Neither Kramer, nor Hornung, nor any of the Packers really cared who drove off with the car. The only thing that mattered was the Packers were the world champs.

All the punishing practices, all the brutal hitting, all the blood and sweat and battered muscles had earned their just reward.

"I didn't care anything about the award," Kramer said. "All that mattered to me or anyone on the team was that we won the championship. That's the way Vince Lombardi taught us to play. That's the way we enjoyed playing the game. Besides, how the hell would I get in and out of a Corvette?"

All of the Packers—in fact, the whole community of Green Bay—were winners that day. It was the first championship game ever played in Green Bay. December 31, 1961, remains the city's most historic day since Wisconsin came up with its first vat of cheese and figured maybe there was a chance to capitalize on the product.

The game was equally historic for the soon-to-explode National Football League. It was billed as football's first "million dollar game."

Between a national television rights fee of $615,000 and ticket revenues of $400,000, based on 40,000 tickets all priced at $10 each, the NFL established a heralded milestone.

The figures seem embarrassingly paltry compared to the billion-dollar marketing madness of today's game. But this was critical to the NFL as it laid a foundation for evolution into the forefront of American fanaticism with professional sports.

And it all took place in a speck on the NFL map called Green Bay, Wisconsin—the smallest market in a league of behemoths and still is today.

The Packers had to use shoehorns to slip the 40,000 fans into City Stadium with its listed capacity of a little more than 37,000 seats. The traffic congestion anticipated by the authorities prompted them to bring in extra police support from four surrounding cities.

"The feeling was indescribable," Kramer said. "Today, there are more than 100,000 people who probably claim to have been at the game."

Green Bay was proud to claim their Packers as a "community project and regional religion." The local chamber of commerce tabbed the city as "Titletown USA" the week before the game was played.

When game day finally arrived, even the weatherman seemed to sparkle with Packer spirit. Although the Packers had practiced that week in temperatures that dipped to minus-10 degrees, by Sunday the thermometer rose to a "pleasant" 20 degrees above zero.

The field remained in magnificently good shape and was regarded to be fast. During the week it was covered by a tarp beneath a layer of hay which then fell under fourteen inches of snow.

Perhaps as a psychological ploy, the Packers ran through their pre-game workout wearing short-sleeved jerseys.

"We wanted to show the Giants that we were comfortable in our house," Kramer said.

The game began under a cloudy sky that finally decided to join the festivities by allowing the sun to break through.

The fans were appreciative, but the Packers probably never noticed. The focus of their mission was immovable. The intensity of their execution was breathtakingly complete.

During the week preceding the game, Vince Lombardi's influence, generated from his coaching tenure at West Point, was rewarded. Hornung, wide receiver Boyd Dowler, and linebacker Ray Nitschke all had been granted leaves from their service in the Army. It allowed the Packers to prepare at full strength.

And the Giants paid the price.

Offensively and defensively, the Packers struck with surgical precision. Despite having only nipped the Giants, 20–17, during the regular season, the Packers swallowed their foes from the league's largest city with total domination in every phase of the game.

The Giants finished the regular season as the team yielding the least amount of points to their opponents. Obviously, the Packers were not the least bit impressed—neither by statistics nor by the reputation of the big bullies from the big city.

The Packers used a running game to open up the passing lanes. They pounded the ball up the middle. They ran the sweep right and left, inside and outside. They dared the Giants to stop it even when they knew it was coming.

After a scoreless first quarter, the Packers erupted for three touchdowns and a field goal in the second period. It was a statement quarter to let the world know that a dynasty had officially begun.

Kramer caught a fourteen-yard pass from Bart Starr untouched in the corner of the end zone for the third touchdown of the quarter. The exquisitely timed play did not resemble Kramer's second catch of the game.

On that play, Kramer grabbed a pass in the middle of the field. He then proceeded to drag what seemed to be half of New York's defenders down the field to set up the first of three Hornung field goals to make the score 24–0 at the half.

"Ron looked like a freight car hauling heavy steel," Hornung said.

In the third quarter Kramer grabbed a thirteen-yard touchdown lob from Starr to put the game out of reach. For the game, Kramer was the leading receiver with four catches and eighty yards.

Even more impressive was his relentless punishing blocking, particularly of All Pro linebacker Sam Huff.

"We had a play where [center Jim] Ringo starts at him," Kramer said. "Then Ringo leaves. Huff is looking at where Ringo is going and I come in and bust him in half. I put him on his butt a few times. He still teases me about that when we run into each other today."

Everything worked to the perfection Lombardi demanded. Even when adversity tried to derail his plan, the Packers quickly compensated.

"Forrest Gregg was probably as good a tackle ever to play in the league," Kramer said. "He and I played well together.

"In that game, [guard] Jerry Kramer got hurt. Fortunately, we had two outstanding left tackles—Bob Skoronski and Norm Masters. Masters switched from left to right tackle and Skoronski moved in to left tackle. Gregg was able to switch to guard. That's how good a team we had."

The Packers were equally dominating on the defensive side of

Vince Lombardi made the players' wives happy with new mink stoles after their husbands won the 1961 NFL championship for Green Bay.

the ball. The Giants' deepest penetration all day was to Green Bay's six-yard line before they had to surrender the ball on downs.

For the victory, each of the Packers earned a little more than $5,000. Sounds paltry compared to today's winning paycheck that runs into the hundreds of thousands. The Giants were compensated with a little more than $3,000 per man.

In addition to the monetary compensation from the league, Lombardi gave each of his players a color television set. He also presented each of the players' wives with a mink stole. It was his way of thanking the wives for the sacrifices they made by allowing their spouses to spend so much time perfecting their talents.

Of course, the rewards were appreciated. Nothing, though, was more gratifying than the championship ring.

"That's what every player plays for," Kramer said. "For us, it not only symbolized a championship, but also the team—the family—that we were all part of."

The victory sent the city into unabated delirium. Although authorities tried to prevent overly zealous fans from tearing down the goal posts, their efforts resembled those of the Giants as the posts came tumbling down.

"Some fans chained them to a car and drove them all around town," Kramer said. "Sparks were flying. It looked like the Fourth of July."

Actually, it was New Year's Eve and Kramer had the opportunity to celebrate the occasion with his entire family. Not only were Mom, Pop, wife Nancy, and son Kurt at the game, so too was daughter Cassie who had been born the previous September shortly after the season began.

Kramer and a few of his happy-go-lucky teammates actually started the party a little earlier in the week.

"We knew we were ready to play the game of our lives," said guard Fuzzy Thurston. "We were together and we could feel it. We partied a little during the week. A lot of people don't know, but Ron and I were both overweight for that game. I don't care what it said in the record book. I weighed 280 and Ron was around 275. But we never let that interfere with what we had to do. We played the best game we ever played."

Hornung, of course, had been a willing early celebrant.

"I remember when Ron showed up, the smell of his breath preceded him," Hornung cracked. "I told him, 'Damn, Ron, don't go near Lombardi.' When Ron got in the huddle Starr almost had a heart attack."

Those were the characters that made the era so special. That was the game that started the train on a roll.

And the message from Hornung was loud and clear—"If you want to get to me, you have to go through Kramer."

18   *"General, This Is Kramer"*

Shortly after the 1991 conclusion of Desert Storm—the United States' lopsided victory over Iraq when Saddam Hussein mistakenly decided to invade Kuwait—Ron Kramer enjoyed a rather unconventional encounter with U.S. Army General H. Norman Schwarzkopf.

As one might expect with anything involving Kramer, the incident was poignantly humorous and one that even the ol' general is not likely to forget.

Kramer was watching a television news show in which the military analyst explained Schwarzkopf's battle plan that sent Hussein's overmatched troops scurrying back to Iraq. The war was an Olympic size mismatch. In terms of football relativity, the decisive victory required less than one quarter.

The battle plan that Schwarzkopf employed looked distinctly familiar to Kramer. The American troops were using tanks, grenades, rocket launchers, and a variety of other military paraphernalia instead of helmets, pads, goal posts, and first down markers used by Kramer and the boys of his profession.

Strangely, however, Kramer was sure he had seen the underlying basics before.

"I sat straight up in my chair," Kramer said. "Son of a bitch! This is the Packer sweep."

Kramer recalled that Schwarzkopf had played football at the United States Military Academy under Coach Red Blaik. One of Blaik's top assistants had been none other than Vince Lombardi.

Kramer couldn't contain himself. Suddenly he felt a kinship with the five-star general that only those who served under Lombardi share. He felt compelled to do something. He decided to

Detroit Lions

P.O. Box 151
Fenton, MI 48430
(313) 629-8788
MICS 9532

March 21, 1991

DIRECTORS

Terry Barr
John Conti
Jim David
Dorne Dibble
John Gonzaga
Bob Hynes
Bob James
Ken Janke
Ron Kramer
Gil Mains
Bill O'Brien
John Panelli
Nick Pietrosante
Joe Schmidt
Tim Sullivan
Tom Watkins
Mike Weger

HALL OF FAME

Jack Christensen
Bill Dudley
John Henry Johnson
"Night Train" Lane
Yale Lary
Bobby Layne
Joe Schmidt
Doak Walker
Alex Wojciechowitz

General Norman Schwarzkopf
Pentagon Building
Arlington, Virginia 22201-99

Dear "BEAR" Sir,

    While intently observing the Desert Storm via
T.V. it became quite obvious that the mission
could not have been completed without the "Schwarz-
koph Sweep". As a member of the Green Bay Packers
it became apparent that "Lombardi's Sweep " and the
"Schwarzkopf Sweep" had many similarties.

    Lombardi must have obsconded with the concept-
ions while assisting Red Blake at West Points. I
am confident that Vince would have approved of the
Schwarzkopf version. Especially it's victorious
results:

    Please accept my congratulations, speaking for
Vince and the Green Bay Packers, you all did a hell
of a job, Thanks

RON KRAMER
GREEN BAY PACKERS
TIGHT END (Retired Expert)

Ron Kramer couldn't resist telling the General himself how proud he was of him for having perfectly executed the celebrated Packers' sweep in a showdown far more serious than any football game.

COMMANDER IN CHIEF
UNITED STATES CENTRAL COMMAND
OPERATION DESERT STORM, APO NY 09852

9 April 1991

Dear Ron,

Thanks for your letter and particularly your great comparison of my battle plan to the "Lombardi Sweep." Vince Lombardi coached me for a while at West Point and I can still remember him demonstrating some techniques to me by hitting me harder without pads than I ever hit anyone with pads.

Jack Kemp wrote me and told me my maneuver really wasn't a Hail Mary play. I explained to him that my version of the Hail Mary is really an illegal play. Instead of wide receivers and flankers I sent out linebackers and tight ends whose only job was to go deep and then jump up and down on the deep defenders. Naturally, this play always results in a penalty, but the opposing team sure thinks twice before they decide to play you in another away game.

Thanks for your great letter.

Sincerely,

H. NORMAN SCHWARZKOPF
General, U.S. Army

Mr. Ron Kramer
DETROIT LIONS
P.O. Box 151
Fenton, MI 48430

The General thanked Kramer for his kindness and reminded him that lessons learned from Lombardi are never forgotten.

write Schwarzkopf a letter commending him on his brilliant plan of attack.

In the letter, Kramer carefully sketched diagrams of both the "Schwarzkopf Sweep" and the "Lombardi Sweep." Both, of course, were unstoppable. He told the general how proud Lombardi would have felt seeing his prize play lifted to a supreme level.

"I suppose the general was pretty busy at the time, but I thought he should know how proud all Americans were of him," Kramer said. "That's just me—one of the crazy things I do."

Kramer wrote the letter on March 21, 1991. Schwarzkopf was swift with his return note of gratitude, dated April 9, 1991.

The letter thanked Kramer for what the general described as high praise. He also assured Kramer that the lessons he learned from Lombardi have never been forgotten and are routinely applied to his daily life.

The sweep, as run by the Packers, did not encompass the serious consequences of the one run by Schwarzkopf. For teams trying to defend Lombardi's version, however, the results were just as convincing.

There are certain icons of sports that remain timeless as the playing of the National Anthem before every game.

No one had to actually witness the 1927 New York Yankees, featuring Babe Ruth and Lou Gehrig, to appreciate the immortality of "Murderer's Row." The old Boston Garden is gone, but memories of that distinct parquet floor still survive. And those not remotely interested in horse racing recognize that the playing of Stephen Foster's "My Old Kentucky Home" signals the start of the annual Kentucky Derby.

Though dormant now for decades, the romance of the Green Bay sweep remains as vibrant as if the Packers had been running it just last year.

More than for its complexity of design, the sweep became nearly unstoppable because of the Packers' surgical execution. That execution, indisputably, was the direct result of discipline and determination.

"The sweep was repetition," Kramer explained. "We ran that play in practice so much we all could see it in our dreams. It's the same thing as reading a book. If you read it and read it and read it, eventually you're going to know what it means. I had a natural gift for sports, but that doesn't mean anything if you don't develop it."

Unlike most teams that run wind sprints to conclude a practice,

Lombardi took diabolical delight in repeatedly running the sweep against the first team defense.

This was the most prolific offense in the league running its crown jewel play against the toughest defense. Lombardi believed if they could make it work in practice, Sunday's execution would feel like a practice without pads.

Over and over again, the two units went nose to nose. Their bodies were expended to the point of becoming familiar with the grunts and groans of the man each was attacking.

Practices were long and bloody. They provided the stiffest test of endurance and determination.

Gary Knafelc was Lombardi's inherited first tight end. A wide receiver playing out of position at 215 pounds, Knafelc could see it was only a matter of time until the stronger and more athletically gifted Kramer reclaimed his health to seize the position.

Until that time, however, Knafelc bravely endured the punishment inflicted upon him by his own linebackers. Thoroughly beaten after having run the play so many times that he lost count, Knafelc brought a smile even to the face of his relentless coach.

"I was like a tennis ball out there getting bounced back and forth," Knafelc recalled. "I finally told Coach Lombardi I think even [linebacker Ray] Nitschke knows the sweep is coming."

In the sweep, no single player's assignment was more important than the one of each of his teammates.

"It was all teamwork," Kramer emphasized. "That was the genius of Lombardi.

"Think of an eight-cylinder engine. If one cylinder goes down, they all go down. It was the same with the sweep. If I don't read the linebacker right, the play breaks down. If the guards don't pull and hit their men, the play breaks down. If the tackles and center don't execute their blocks, the play breaks down. If the running backs don't follow the blocks and hit the holes, the play breaks down."

Left guard Fuzzy Thurston concurs with Kramer's analysis. He adds one distinction, however, to underscore Lombardi's contention that Kramer added the dimension of a twelfth man.

"It was a play where everyone had to do his job or it didn't work," Thurston said. "If one man failed, everyone failed. Even if the other team knew the sweep was coming, if we executed properly they couldn't stop it. The play demanded teamwork. Every play, though, has a trigger. No block was more important than Kramer's."

Quarterback Bart Starr also concurs.

"Ron was the best tight end blocker," Starr said. "Every block in the sweep was critical to make it work properly. His block was critical because everything fed off of it."

Kramer's block in the sweep was an upright one that actually determined how the play would unfold. It demanded as much brain as brawn and the will to make it happen regardless of the situation.

Kramer's assignment actually started when he lined up on the line of scrimmage. The sweep demanded a thirty-inch split between tackle Forrest Gregg and himself. Lombardi was paranoid about the extra six inches that were not required on other plays. In practice, he would stop the play before it was run if he felt the split was not precisely six inches.

"Precise spacing was important because if the linebacker was going to blitz down the line of scrimmage, I was still able to block him down and the sweep went around him," Kramer explained. "If the linebacker makes penetration into the backfield, he can disrupt the play because he knocks down the pulling guards and everybody else can make the tackle because there's no blocking in front of [Paul] Hornung or [Jim] Taylor."

Once the ball was snapped, Kramer had to make a split second decision as to whether the linebacker was going inside or outside. As soon as the linebacker made the slightest move, Kramer blocked him in the same direction and the play was run into the open area.

"Ron can downplay it or say anything he wants, but the absolute key to the success of the sweep was his block," Hornung said. "If he didn't take the linebacker out, nothing else mattered. The guard and I were keying on that block and if it wasn't there, it was all over."

Once Kramer's block was delivered, the guard and the runner could determine whether the play should be run inside or outside.

Hornung had won the Heisman Trophy playing quarterback for Notre Dame. Hornung's running ability, balance, and football street sense led Lombardi to switch him to halfback for the play he had envisioned.

To make the play work, though, Lombardi needed the precise personnel at every position. Kramer's ability to single block and double as a receiving threat was as critical to the play's success as Hornung's ability to run to daylight.

"The play doesn't work without Ron," Hornung said flatly.

The rest of his teammates agree.

"Ron just had a sense for which way the linebacker was moving—inside or outside," Thurston said. "I never worried about anybody getting into the backfield with Ron out there."

Neither did any of the other Packers who marveled at Kramer's ability to read and throw blocks.

"Ron must have blocked at ninety percent every week," said wide receiver Boyd Dowler. "He won all the awards Lombardi handed out. The linebacker would try to sneak inside of Kramer and that just didn't happen. He owned the linebackers. He could handle a defensive end by himself."

Now an assistant coach in the NFL, Dowler can appreciate even more why Lombardi was so passionate about the sweep.

"We had the perfect blend of people for it," Dowler said. "It worked because we had the people to make it work that other teams didn't. We had guards who could pull and we had Kramer at tight end who could single block. The tight end was critical in the sweep."

The eyes and handshake still say "friends for life," as Vince Lombardi and Ron Kramer salute each other briefly after Kramer played his first game against his former teammates after being traded to the Detroit Lions.

Former Detroit Lions' middle linebacker Joe Schmidt was the recipient of more Kramer blocks than he cares to remember.

"That was a critical block Kramer had in the sweep," Schmidt said. "It didn't matter to him whether he was taking out a linebacker or a defensive end. That man could flat out block."

As impressive to Schmidt as Kramer's physical abilities were, more so were the intangibles he brought to the game every time he stepped onto the field.

"Kramer was blessed with a lot of talent," Schmidt said. "I can see why whatever he tries, he's going to be the best because he had a passion to be nothing less.

"But he also had an innate feel for the game. You can't see a lot of the intangibles he brought to the game. They didn't show up in the statistics or the record book. But he knew what he was doing out there every play of the game."

The sweep became a trademark for the Packers as much as the green and gold of their helmets. Kramer perceives the sweep as much more than merely another successful football play.

"The sweep is the epitome of teamwork," Kramer said. "If Hornung or Taylor scored a touchdown, it didn't belong just to them. It belonged to everyone on the field. If just one of those guys hadn't done his job, then no one would have gotten the ball into the end zone."

For Kramer, the play also symbolizes something bigger than a football game.

"Think about it," Kramer demanded. "Doesn't that play represent what America is supposed to be all about? Aren't we supposed to be a team? How can any team be successful if everyone isn't contributing to it?

"We have to learn how to work together. I get so tired of hearing people say, 'I've got to do my own thing.' If their 'own thing' doesn't help everybody, then what the hell good is it? We're in this thing together and we better straighten things out."

Apparently, the strategy was good enough for Schwarzkopf to make his point with Iraq.

And the way Kramer figures, if it was good enough for Lombardi, it was good enough for the general. And if it was good enough for him, then it at least deserves a letter of recognition from one of the key elements who made the concept work.

At least that's the way Kramer sees it.

19   *Those Lovable Packers*

Dear Abby:
I have a problem ... I have two brothers. One brother plays for the Green Bay Packers and the other one is sentenced to die in the electric chair. My mother died from insanity when I was three years old. My two sisters are prostitutes (one has AIDS) and my father sells drugs. I recently met a girl who was released from a reformatory where she served time for smothering her illegitimate child. I love this girl and want to marry her. My problem is this ... should I tell her about my brother who plays for the Packers?

This parody of the popular syndicated newspaper advice column has been lying in Ron Kramer's office for years. He doesn't remember and it doesn't matter how he got it. Once he did, he duplicated several copies to give to his former teammates.

They appreciate a good laugh about the brotherhood they still share today.

Kramer amuses himself by collecting offbeat knickknacks, pictures, and a myriad of unexplainable doodads. Anything, really, that provokes a smile.

"Why not?" he asks matter-of-factly. "One of the problems we have in the world now is that we've forgotten how to laugh. Some people ought to get the stick out of their butts and learn that life is meant to be lived. Besides, we [the Packers] didn't do that many bad things ... did we?"

Not only did Vince Lombardi's Packers enjoy a reputation for being a relentlessly precise, disemboweling scourge on the field, some of their off-field adventures must have found their way into some kind of hall of fame of their own.

"After the game Sunday till the Tuesday morning meeting were the fun times for us," said wide receiver Max McGee. "From the end of that game till Tuesday morning it was wine, women and song ... maybe Saturday nights, too, when we were on the road."

Despite their time under the neon lights, however, McGee added that they were always ready to play.

"We spent some time in the bars," he said. "But we were in good condition. Playing for Lombardi, you had to be in good condition."

Kramer still savors the memories.

"We did enjoy ourselves," he admits. "Lots of memories. Lots of good times. But never at the expense of the team."

And the question is—why shouldn't they have enjoyed themselves?

The Packers of the 1960s were a collection of some of the most magnificent athletes on the face of the planet. They were young, virile, handsome, educated. They were champions in a profession that is the measure of masculinity, playing a game that sat on the brink of rewriting television sports history.

And most of them, quite simply, loved life as much as the games they played.

"Lombardi understood the situation," Kramer said. "He knew we were virile young men. He knew the perks and pitfalls for successful young football players. He also knew how to deal with it. That's how smart he was."

Several stories appeared in the local media suggesting it wasn't necessary for fans to spend their money on tickets to a Packers' game. They could see their stars free of charge by simply visiting select local pubs throughout the week.

The players offered no apologies. None were necessary. They were content to let the record book stand as their judge.

"Did we hurt anybody?" Kramer asks. "No. Did we fool around with drugs and weapons like we read about athletes doing today? No. Did our names appear on as many police blotters as sports pages? No. Were we disciplined and make the most of our talent on the field? Yes. Did we enjoy ourselves along the way? Absolutely yes!"

Lombardi certainly didn't live in a cave, oblivious to the stories that swirled around a band of his players. He regularly received letters and phone calls from vigilant Green Bay residents depicting certain nocturnal habits of his celebrated charges.

The coach was wise. More than the Xs and Os of a playbook, he understood young football players. He was that special kind of leader who could handle a myriad of personalities like a magician does a deck of cards.

"People used to ask if we had the perfect blend of personalities," Kramer said. "I think we had the perfect 'un-blend.' We had so many different personalities, but we had the perfect blender. That was Lombardi. He brought us all together."

Lombardi was smart enough to know everything that transpired on his team and wise enough to appreciate the difference between dealing with trouble and looking for it.

Kramer explained that the coaches enjoyed their happy hours, too. An unwritten rule, however, prohibited each member of the team from frequenting the preferred relaxation establishment of those on the coaching side.

"Let's put it this way," Kramer said, showing his own flash of wisdom. "Lombardi knew all the places where not to go. He knew everything. He didn't care what you did as long as you were doing your job. You just better be ready to go at it hard the next day or, for sure, you would hear from him."

Even on the road, players were aware of the coaches' preferred spots for dinner and cocktails. Coaches, in turn, had a good idea of where their players might be doing their own brand of relaxing.

In Green Bay, no one needed a program to know where players chose to "relax" after practice.

Lombardi's rule for drinking in public places was never to be seen sitting at the bar.

"I'm not sure why he had that rule," Kramer said. "He didn't mind drinks on the table, but he felt drinking at the bar just didn't look professional."

Ray Nitschke felt the bite of Lombardi's law when the coach and a few of his assistants wandered into a Santa Monica pub where the Hall of Famer was drinking alone at the bar. Nitschke didn't try to hide. In fact, he sent the coaches a round of drinks.

It may have been a noble attempt at survival through reverse psychology. He was dealing, however, with the master psychologist and now the enforcer of the law he had established.

Lombardi exploded and decided to settle the matter at a team meeting the next day. He told his men he was ready to suspend the All Pro linebacker, but would leave it up to a team vote.

"Lombardi knew what he was doing," Kramer laughed. "He knew we needed the guy. Nitschke was a helluva player, but Vince had to find a way to make his rule stick. He was smart. He knew we weren't going to vote Nitschke out. So he took a vote and let the process run a little long just to make Nitschke sweat."

The psychology worked and Nitschke outplayed himself the following Sunday against the Rams.

"Nitschke was one mean and ornery character," Kramer said. "He loved to fight. When he quit drinking, though, he became the poster child for the ideal Green Bay Packer. I loved the guy."

Kramer was indirectly involved with another bar sitting incident.

In Chicago before the Packers played the season-opening College All-Star Game, Paul Hornung and a date were seated at the bar of the Red Carpet waiting for Kramer and his wife to arrive for dinner. Even though Kramer was late, Hornung apparently considered the establishment to be coach-free.

Surprisingly, Lombardi happened to arrive. And so did the fireworks that ended with a two hundred-and-fifty-dollar fine.

"When we got there, the waiter told us that Lombardi had gone ballistic," Kramer laughed. "He told us to meet Paul at the Pump Room."

When Kramer arrived, Hornung was seated at a table nursing a martini.

"I think that was one of the few times Paul said: 'You buy the dinner—this one already has cost me two-fifty,'" Kramer chuckled.

California seemed to be a spot where trouble had a peculiar knack for finding unsuspecting players. Kramer and Boyd Dowler felt the sting of the Golden State following the 1963 season-ending Saturday game in San Francisco.

The Packers decided to spend the evening in San Francisco and return to Green Bay on Sunday. Gary Crosby, son of the famous singer and movie star Bing Crosby, invited a few of the Packers to a party on Saturday evening. Kramer doesn't remember where the party was or who all the guests were.

"All I know is we got whacked," he said. "The party went on all night. Boyd Dowler and I finally passed out on a couple of chairs."

When Kramer groggily came back to life, about thirty people were still partying from the night before. He peeked through the blinds and felt his eyes pierced by the shining sun. On a TV in the corner of the room, he noticed the Detroit Lions playing the Chicago Bears in a game to determine the conference championship. A Bears' victory would send them to the title game. A loss would give the conference to the Packers.

Kramer immediately felt blindsided as if hit by a blitzing linebacker.

"We got trouble," Kramer told Dowler while trying to revive his still sleeping teammate.

Kramer told Crosby he had to get them to the airport faster than any Hornung touchdown run.

Crosby did his best, but the mad dash was fruitless. The Packers' charter flight had already departed.

Kramer scurried to purchase tickets for himself and Dowler to take them to Chicago for a connecting flight to Green Bay.

Ironically, the Packers' plane encountered a few delays that allowed enough time for the pair of miscreants to actually beat the team home.

Nevertheless, when the pair reported to Lombardi the following morning, the coach was still irate. The fact that Chicago beat Detroit to clinch the title certainly didn't help.

Lombardi fined each player five hundred dollars, in addition to the cost of the airline tickets.

"But the season is over," Kramer pleaded his case to the coach and final judge.

"Five hundred dollars!" Lombardi closed the case.

Was the party worth it?

"Let's just say like that television commercial—some things are priceless," Kramer said with a smile.

It was a good time to be a Green Bay Packer.

20 *The Only Choice*

Sometimes the toughest decision is the easiest to make, especially in matters pertaining to values and principle.

Ron Kramer faced the biggest decision of his life following the 1964 season. The choice he made left a lot of players and fans alike asking themselves the same question: Given a similar situation, would I have the guts to make the same call?

"It wasn't that hard because it was the right thing to do," he explained. "If I hadn't done it, I would have gone against everything I believe in."

Still in his prime and an integral part of the celebrated Green Bay Packers offense, Kramer suddenly made the decision to walk away.

This was not just another NFL team he was leaving. Under legendary coach Vince Lombardi, the Packers established themselves as one of history's legitimate dynasties.

Following three straight conference championships and back-to-back NFL titles in 1961 and 1962, the Packers finished second in 1963 and 1964. Still, they were armed with the nucleus of what was to become one of the most historic runs in football history.

The Packers captured another NFL title in 1965 and then won the first two Super Bowls in 1966 and 1967 after the NFL merged with the American Football League.

Kramer could have finished his already distinguished career with five championship rings instead of two. Almost certainly, his ticket into the Football Hall of Fame would have been assured.

"I think Lombardi respected Ron even more when he explained why he had to go to Detroit," said Hall of Famer Paul Hornung. "If a deal couldn't have been worked out with Detroit, Ron would have retired.

"He could have stuck with the Packers and won three more championship rings. He still should be in the Hall of Fame. He and Mike Ditka are the two best tight ends to have played the game. But Ron had to do what he believed was right. That took guts and class. But that's Ron Kramer."

Despite all of the consequences to his career, Kramer chose to walk away. And he never spent a single moment looking back.

The Packers had forged Kramer's identity. They provided a lifestyle in professional sports that only a few are privileged to taste. The Packers provided more than a profession. For Kramer, they had become a passion.

Only one thing was more precious.

"Nothing is more important than family," he still insists. "Not the Packers. Not championships. Not the Hall of Fame. Nothing. My parents taught me that a long time ago. Lombardi preached it all the time. With him it was God, family, and the Packers."

A number of factors figured into Kramer's decision to leave Green Bay. His son, Kurt, had lost significant sight in one eye that had been gouged by a pair of scissors. His daughter, Cassie, was suffering from serious bouts with asthma. And his marriage to first wife, Nancy, had fallen into a nosedive that resembled the Packers' seasons before the arrival of Lombardi.

"One time I came home and my five-year-old daughter slept on my chest for three straight nights," Kramer said. "The doctor had given her the wrong prescription and she was hallucinating. She thought the street lights outside were giant bugs coming to attack her."

Kramer phoned the doctor who instructed him to bring her to the office in the morning.

"I told him we would be there in an hour and they better be ready for us," Kramer said. "If you're not, I'll bust down the door."

Cassie was treated that evening, but the incident convinced Kramer that it was time for him to be at home.

"I'm not sure a lot of people realize the professional price Ron paid for making that decision," said former teammate Gary Knafelc. "He was a Hall of Fame player. He just didn't play long enough with the Packers to be elected. He made the decision because he believed it was the right thing to do. How many guys would have had the guts to pay that price? It tells you the caliber of his character."

Kramer had developed into the perfect tight end for Lombardi's offense. He could block. He could catch. He could run with defenders half his size. Most importantly, Kramer had a feel for the game. He was one of the most disciplined players in the game. He was Lombardi's twelfth man on the field.

While Lombardi asked Kramer to reconsider his decision, he assured his prime tight end that he understood.

"He told me that he couldn't replace me," Kramer said. "He also told me that he understood. He said if anything were to change to give him a call."

When Lombardi was convinced Kramer's decision was final, he arranged a deal with Detroit allowing Kramer to go to his hometown Lions in exchange for a draft choice. That selection turned out to be Jim Grabowski, a bruising running back out of the University of Illinois who wound up playing on three Packer championship teams.

"Every time I run into him now, he thanks me and holds up three fingers in front of me," Kramer laughed.

If the Packers and Lions couldn't have arranged the deal, Kramer was prepared to retire. Grabowski certainly is grateful that the transaction went through.

Kramer is the first to admit that he would never be mistaken for Ozzie Nelson, the All-American father figure portrayed by the late actor during the infancy of TV sitcoms.

But nothing—not even the aura of the powerful Green Bay Packers—stood above the love he feels for his children.

"Maybe a lot of people were surprised by his decision," said Kramer's sister, Anna Marie, "but not me. Ron was always close to his kids. He's close to his whole family. That's the way we were raised. Family always came first."

Cassie now is married to Brian Koehler. The couple lives in Orlando with two of Kramer's three grandchildren—Heidi, 21, and Kurt, 18. Being a mother and the daughter of a celebrated professional star, Cassie now can place perspective on the decision her father made.

"I was too young to understand what had happened at the time," Cassie said. "But putting everything together, I'm so proud of the decision my father made."

She paused for a moment and then smiled while recalling Grandma Adeline.

"I'm not surprised, though," Cassie continued. "Family means everything to him. He loves my brother and me to death. He loves his grandchildren. That's the way he was raised. He was a mama's boy. I was very close to my grandmother and my dad got a lot from her. Grandma was sassy. She always let you know exactly what she was thinking. But she was fair and open-minded. It was always family first. We were very close friends."

Kurt concurs with his sister's perception.

"No doubt about it," said Kurt, who is married to Dawn and is the father of Kramer's third grandchild, Kelsey, 16.

"Dad was a mama's boy. Grandma absolutely adored him. For her, he could do no wrong.

"I was glad when Dad came back to Detroit. He got involved with me playing hockey and all my other sports. A lot of people question how much he cares about things that really matter. He portrays something different than he really is. He comes off harsh and gruff allowing things to roll off his back. He's much more sensitive than people realize. He roars pretty loud, but he's so much softer inside. Looking back, it doesn't surprise me about the decision he made. He's a man of integrity and it was the right thing to do."

Playing for the Lions, however, was similar to returning to Baghdad after spending a vacation in the Caribbean.

There were a few similarities between the Packers and the Lions. Both played in the NFL. Both played their games on Sunday afternoons. Neither was allowed to put more than eleven men on the field at the same time. And both played the same amount of preseason exhibition and regular season games.

The Packers, of course, always continued to play once the regular season ended. The Lions got an early start on "waiting till next year."

"The biggest difference was attitude," Kramer said. "There was a winning attitude in Green Bay and a total losing attitude in Detroit."

It was as apparent as new cars rolling down Detroit's busy assembly lines.

"I knew all the players before I got there," Kramer said. "Terry Barr and I played at Michigan together and used to run around during off-seasons. They were all good guys, but didn't have the leadership I was used to at Green Bay. There was so much controversy between [coach] Harry Gilmer and the players it was incredible. Nobody cared one way or the other.

"Everybody was running helter-skelter because there was no organization. Guys didn't get along. The offense and the defense were like Israel and Iran. There were so many factions. I had just come from Vince Lombardi and the best organization in the game. I knew what I was getting into, but until you get into a fire you don't know how hot it really is."

Middle linebacker Joe Schmidt wound up succeeding Gilmer as coach after Kramer retired.

"I never knew the details about Ron's coming home to Detroit," Schmidt said. "But I don't think Harry [Gilmer] wanted the trade. He tried to make a defensive end out of Kramer. I know he could have been a good one. He probably could have played almost any position. But why tinker with a great tight end?"

Kramer played through 1967 for the Lions and never tasted a winning season. They went 6-7-1 in 1965, 4-9-1 in 1966, and 5-7-2 in 1967.

Kramer played all fourteen games in each of the 1965 and 1966 seasons. He caught eighteen passes in 1965 and thirty-seven in 1966. He played eleven games and caught four passes in 1967 before announcing his retirement.

"I never looked back and thought what could have been if I had stayed in Green Bay," Kramer said. "After you make a decision, you move on. What's the sense in playing 'what if' games? There are new challenges to deal with."

Kramer used his time in Detroit to enhance his other profession. He was a minority owner in Paragon Steel and was savvy enough to capitalize on his unique public persona. He regularly brought customers to the park for close-up looks during practice. He left tickets to Sunday home games for key clients and then joined them for a post-game meal. Regardless of the state of the Lions, inside looks at a professional sports team were a sales incentive that competing representatives could not offer.

"It worked great from that perspective, but there was no comparison between Green Bay and Detroit on the field," Kramer said. "What the hell ... I was fortunate to have tasted the good times."

Most important to Kramer was the additional time he got to spend with his kids at home.

"I have no regrets," he said. "I knew what I was getting into before I went there. I made the right decision for the right reasons. I'd make the same decision today."

Not long ago, Kramer received a letter from a young fan in Superior, Wisconsin, who had not even been born during the heyday of Lombardi's Packers. It touched Kramer enough to save it with other meaningful reminders of his career.

The letter reads:

> *Dear Mr. Kramer,*
>
> *I hope this letter finds you well. I am writing because I am a huge Packer fan (of course). Ever since I was a kid— not all that long ago—I have enjoyed reading about & writing to former GB Packers who have made significant contributions to the Packer organization. The internet has provided me with an abundance of information to choose from. Technology has made it so much easier for fans to enjoy looking up GB Packer news—new & old. In the last couple of months, I read an article about you, in fact. In addition to speaking about your on the field accolades, the article also discussed your decision to go back to Michigan for your family. I was impressed by your integrity. Yet it seems like you are an example of many others from that era who demonstrated good character. In today's fast-paced "Terrell Owens"—type of NFL, it sure is great to be able to read about the "Good Old Days." Even though I wasn't alive during the 60's, I've learned a lot about life & integrity from the Packer players from your era. Thank you for being part of that.*
>
> *Mr. Kramer, if it wouldn't be too much to ask, would you mind signing the enclosed index card I made? It would be an honor to have your signature as part of my Green Bay Packers collection. Thank you for your consideration & I really hope I hear from you.*

Does it really matter that Kramer decided to leave the glitz and glory of the Green Bay Packers during one of the most colorful eras in the history of professional sports?

It certainly does to Kurt and Cassie Kramer. The same goes for that young Green Bay fan in Superior, Wisconsin.

And who knows? Maybe to a lot of others who believe there are more important things in life than football games and championships.

For Kramer, the toughest decision of his life turned out to be quite easy. Without thinking about it for a second, he would do it again and again and again.

21   *Keeping Family First*

Ron Kramer vividly recalls the day he returned home from a business trip and did a double take to make sure he had walked into the right house.

"Something looks different here," he said to himself.

It almost looked surreal.

Except for his golf clubs, his toothbrush, and maybe a bar of soap, everything was gone.

"I mean everything!" he said emphatically. "The furniture was gone. The kids were gone. All the birds were gone. I never knew she could make a house look so clean."

If it wasn't nailed down, it was gone, he declared.

For a couple of years after Kramer retired from the Detroit Lions, he and Nancy tried to save their marriage.

"After seeing the house that day, I kind of got the idea that we weren't going to make it," he understated.

Nancy had taken everything back to her parents' home in Cassopolis, Michigan, about a three-and-a-half hour drive from Detroit. That's where she and the kids stayed while the divorce ran its course.

Divorce day was another one Kramer will always remember.

Appearing before the judge, Kramer was shocked by Nancy's claim that he had physically abused her. Kramer intently eyed the judge.

"Your honor," Kramer calmly stated his case. "Would you kindly look at this beautiful lady? She's maybe 110 pounds. Am I not more than double her size? I was a professional athlete. I was trained to hit people. If I had abused her, I'd have her hanging up over my mantel."

The judge quickly denied the allegation and granted the divorce.

Even divorce has a slice of humor in the world according to Kramer.

"Nancy was a beautiful lady," Kramer said. "I mean drop-dead beautiful—straight out of *Vogue*. When she walked down the street, heads started spinning. That's the way I met her back when we were at the University of Michigan.

"After the judge made it official, I took her to lunch. We shared a couple of bottles of champagne. I told her that she came in this way and she's going out this way. Then we got a room and made love. What the hell? Just because you're not married anymore doesn't mean you can't be friends. The divorce was probably as much my fault as anyone's, but things happen."

Years later Kramer's second marriage to Pam also ended in divorce. The two had lived together for years before giving marriage a shot.

"I think I finally decided it was wiser to be friends with a woman than get into all the legal stuff," Kramer said. "If you really love someone, what's the difference? Even if you break up then, you can still love that person. I still love a lot of women even if I don't see them anymore."

While married to Nancy, Kramer had paid $83,000 for the house in Bloomfield Hills, an affluent suburb northwest of Detroit. In today's market, the house would be priced somewhere around one million dollars.

"I have to laugh when I think about it," he said. "What are you going to do? If someone had purchased a hundred shares of IBM stock way back when, they'd be living on an island in the South Pacific now. It's only money. Life goes on. You have to make the best of it. I didn't lose the one thing that was most important to me."

Kramer's two most precious treasures were—and still remain—his son and daughter—Kurt and Cassie.

Just because marriages fail, families don't have to be destroyed, Kramer reasons. He and Nancy (now deceased) worked diligently to raise their children the right way despite the fact all were not living in the same house.

"We got along well," Kramer said. "We didn't use the kids as a wedge between us. It [the divorce] actually helped our relationship with our children. We made sure to do things right. Every Christmas, every birthday, every graduation, every holiday we all spent together. If there was an important family affair, we shared it together. The relationship we both kept with the kids was wonderful."

Kramer also was committed to keeping the relationship between his kids and his own parents strong and healthy.

"They were not only our kids," he said. "Their grandparents loved them so much. After my dad died, Mom used to take Kurt to the Michigan football games."

When Michigan played in the Rose Bowl one year, Kurt and Grandma Adeline wanted to go to Pasadena.

"Mom told me Kurt wanted to go," Kramer smiled. "I think she wanted to go a little more than Kurt. She called and asked me to get two tickets. She also asked me to make the travel arrangements. She said she'd send me a check. I'm still waiting for it."

The same thing happened when Grandma Adeline decided to take Cassie to Austria to visit where the Kramer family originated. She had Kramer make the arrangements.

"I think that check got lost, too," he smiled. "It didn't matter. I wanted them to know their grandparents the same way I got to know mine."

Kurt and Cassie absolutely adored Grandma Adeline.

"We actually became very close friends," Cassie said.

While the kids lived with Nancy in Cassopolis, Kramer made the three-and-a-half hour drive each Friday to pick them up for the weekend. He turned right around that evening and made the trip back to Detroit. He made the same trip on Sundays to return them.

"The divorce was a difficult time for Dad," Kurt said. "I think he figured that he lost his wife and he wasn't going to lose his kids. He made things happen to stay with us. He did a fantastic job of keeping us together."

Although she was young at the time, Cassie now appreciates her father's determination to keep the family healthy and vibrant.

"He's strong, soft-hearted, and extremely focused," she said. "When he sets his mind on something, he gets it done. You don't see him getting stopped by any obstacles. You don't want him on the other side.

"I never doubted how much he loves me. I appreciate the fact that he didn't start another family like some men do."

As Cassie grew older, she came to appreciate her father even more. Sometimes it's difficult for children to grow up like other kids when their father is the center of public attention.

"I was proud of Dad, but I never understood why everyone seemed to know him," she said. "I remember going to football games at Tiger Stadium and taking my Barbie doll with me. I do wish we could have done things like go to dinner without everyone asking for his autograph and wanting to talk to him. You know how much Dad loves to talk."

While Cassie was in high school, a serious strain developed between her and her mother. She called her father, who was out of town on business.

"She wanted to know if she could live with me," Kramer said.

At the time, Kramer shared his house with live-in girlfriend Gayle Crick.

Kramer, of course, welcomed the opportunity, and called Gayle to pick up his daughter. When he returned, he established the Kramer house rules. Cassie had to maintain good study habits. A zero tolerance curfew for returning home at night was firmly set.

"I could have gone by 'Lombardi time,'" Kramer said. "Whenever he set a time for a team meeting, he expected everyone to show up fifteen minutes early. That was considered prep time. Cassie didn't have to do that. But if she didn't call and showed up a minute late, there was trouble."

Obviously, the new arrangement was successful. Cassie proceeded to graduate from Michigan State University just as her brother had.

She also developed what has turned out to be a lifelong relationship with Gayle, who moved on to marry after graduating summa cum laude with an MBA from the University of Michigan. Now close to retirement after a successful business career and with her own family, she remains close friends with Cassie.

"I owe Gayle so much for her persistent support and friendship to Cassie," Kramer said. "Gayle is a very beautiful, intelligent, and successful lady. We still talk occasionally. I help her get tickets when she wants to go to a big game. Like I said, just because things don't work out between a man and a woman, there's no reason why they can't remain friends."

Nothing is more important to Kramer than family and friends. Both Kurt and Cassie are blessed to have learned that lesson through experience.

Kramer is proud of his kids and feels secure about the life paths they have chosen. Apparently, the experience paid off for Kramer, too.

22 *Never Look Back*

Professional football sometimes tends to be anomalous to civilized society.

While the artistry of a perfectly executed pass play can be appreciated for its timing, touch, and coordinated delicacy, the inherent principles of the game border on the medieval.

Victory is often determined by the simplest of all tenets—which team hit the hardest more times than the other.

It's a game in which the infliction of pain not only is tolerated, it's encouraged and taught as the sure road to success. Adherence to the rules is naturally demanded. Digressions are penalized and often lead to defeat.

But the synchronized mayhem that occurs every Sunday is always accompanied by the possibility that victory will come at some price of adversity.

Sometimes adversity can be severe. One unsuspected block can end a player's career. Depending on degree of intensity, it can cripple for life.

A player's career is always one down away from sudden finality. Adversity lurks closer than the next yard line.

In a world as vicious as professional football, one had better learn how to deal with adversity or save a whole lot of time and energy by simply slipping out the back door.

Ron Kramer learned that basic fact of NFL life from a single hit in 1957. He spent more than two years rehabilitating from a career-threatening injury before fully recovering to reach the promise he always held.

By attacking adversity and refusing to surrender, Kramer was rewarded with a successful NFL career. In sports, wins and losses are the general yardsticks for measuring success. It's plain and simple. More wins than losses determine the degree of success.

Real life unfolds with a lot less clarity. Sometimes the way one reacts to adversity is a more accurate measure of success than the final result itself.

After completing his football career, Kramer was blasted by a double-barrel dose of adversity that had the potential to paralyze someone with less determination. Like the reaction to his career-threatening football injury, however, Kramer's response eventually led to success.

"It's phenomenal how he rolls with adversity," remarked son Kurt Kramer. "A lot of people would have panicked in his situation. Maybe he did inside, but he never showed it."

The situation Kurt referred to was as devastating to Kramer's post-football professional career as the knee injury was to his playing career.

The steel company for which Kramer worked, and in which he actually held a 15 percent ownership, went bankrupt. At about the same time, an upscale restaurant in which Kramer had invested also had to put a lock on the door.

"He is such an optimist," Kurt said. "He didn't let it get him down. If you had gone to dinner with him, you'd never know all the bad stuff that was going on in his life."

There was plenty going on. Not only did he lose a significant amount of money, he also lost a serious investment of time during which he had helped to turn Paragon Steel into a thriving Detroit area enterprise.

Kramer joined the company while still playing for the Packers. His involvement increased after he joined the Lions. Paragon was a steel warehouse company servicing the auto industry. He was an energetic sales representative with the savvy to leverage his influence as a big-time football star.

"My dad was really sharp that way," Kurt said. "He never went around telling anybody who he was. In those days he didn't have to. He worked hard and was able to get through doors a whole lot easier than the competition just because of his name."

Once he joined the Lions, he was able to take key customers to a practice or game as an added sales incentive.

Kramer devised a way to add more punch to the Paragon lineup. He added other local sports figures like the Detroit Tigers' Bill Freehan and Art Houtteman, the Detroit Pistons' Dave Bing, the Detroit Red Wings' Alex Delvecchio, and the Detroit Lions' and Heisman Trophy winner Howard "Hop-a-Long" Cassady to the sales staff.

Kramer also used his offbeat personality to enhance his salesmanship to produce more revenue.

Glenn Wagner was a purchaser of steel through Paragon. He was a horse lover and lived on a farm in Kentucky. Wagner used to tease Kramer about being a "big city boy" trying to out-slicker a boy from the country. On one of his calls to Wagner, Kramer showed up wearing a T-shirt and bib overalls.

"I come from a real farm in Pittsburg, Kansas," Kramer told him. "So don't tell me I don't know anything about the country."

The two remain close friends today and still smile about Kramer's unusually casual business approach. That approach resulted not only in business success, but also in lifelong friendships that Kramer values far more than any amount of sales.

Ed Elliott's friendship with Kramer now runs more than forty

Ron Kramer (*second from left*) recruited athletes like Green Bay receiver Boyd Dowler (*left*) and Detroit Tiger pitcher Art Houtteman (*third from left*) to work with him at Paragon Steel, along with Nance Vacca.

years. Now retired and living in Hendersonville, North Carolina, Elliott used to purchase steel from Kramer.

"It didn't matter that he was a big football star," Elliott said. "The bottom line is that he's a genuine person—a real man's man. Sometimes he'll say things a little too directly, but what he says is always the truth. He's like a brother."

Business was booming for Paragon Steel until the economy took a nosedive like a hundred-pound anchor. Internal disarray resulting from the passing of family ownership to second generation wound up with the company folding.

"Ron was outstanding and a tireless worker," said Errol Peschel who was hired under Kramer. "He knew the business and had a way of making the customers feel good."

Peschel also was treated to an unexpected piece of prime time Kramer hospitality after relocating from New York to join the company.

"I didn't know anything about the city," Peschel recalled. "Ron just said: 'You're coming to my house … no questions asked.' I stayed there, rent-free, for about a year. Ron is extremely generous and loyal. He's the kind of guy you can always count on."

Peschel moved into Kramer's Bloomfield Hills home, which was completely devoid of furniture following his divorce. The divorce was a particularly painful adversity that Kramer also was fighting his way through at the time.

"I went out and bought a mattress and slept on the floor," Peschel laughed. "Those were great times."

Not only had Kramer sacrificed a lot of time toward the building of the company, he also had invested a significant amount of money when allowed to purchase into ownership. Kramer remembers the support he received from his father during his particular time of turmoil.

"I remember telling my dad I had lost a lot of money," Kramer said. "Then he reminded me of something I'll never forget. He asked me how much money I had when I started out. I told him nothing. He said, 'Then what have you lost?'"

Sounds simple, but Kramer certainly appreciated the depth of Pop's words.

Kramer wasted no time getting involved with a variety of diverse projects. One involved serving as a color analyst for the telecast of Detroit Lions' preseason exhibition games with veteran Detroit sportscaster Ray Lane. Lane still treasures one particularly rainy night in Baltimore during which Kramer sent him into a hysterical fit of on-camera laughter.

"The booth we were in really wasn't covered," Lane said. "It rained the entire second quarter. We were drenched. The rain also destroyed all of our charts and statistics. When the camera zoomed in on Ron for his halftime analysis, he held up the dripping chart with running ink and said, 'Well, I guess you can see the first half was mostly running plays.' I cracked up and couldn't stop laughing. Johnny Unitas was in the next booth. He laughed so hard we could hear him on our pickup."

Kramer and Lane still laugh about the incident when they meet today.

"My dad has a knack for putting a shield around him," Kurt said. "He told me that adversity doesn't sting him any less than everyone else. He just doesn't show it."

Once Paragon folded, Kramer founded his own company, appropriately named Ron Kramer Industries. At first, he still brokered steel deals, but also added a wide line of sales incentive items popular with large and small companies for their customers.

"After Paragon folded, I believe Dad actually had a couple of his better financial years," Kurt said.

Money, however, has never been the driving force of Kramer's life. He's much more focused on family, friends, and living each day as if it were his last.

"When it comes to money," Kurt said, "Dad only needs enough to pick up the dinner tab for his friends."

That says it all.

23 *Giving Something Back*

While sorting through personal belongings following the death of his mother, Ron Kramer stumbled across a letter he didn't know existed. The letter, addressed to Mrs. Adeline Kramer, was short, straightforward, sincere, and signed by one of college football's true legends—Woody Hayes. The letter, dated May 27, 1982, reads:

> *Dear Mrs. Kramer:*
> *Thank you very much for your thoughtful letter regarding the Ohio State-Michigan rivalry. It has always been my feeling that it is the greatest rivalry in football and your son certainly helped to make it that way. You know he and I have become real good friends. I hope you say hello to him for me.*
> *Thanks again for your thoughtfulness.*
> *Gratefully yours,*
> *W. W. Hayes*

Kramer has no idea what prompted his mother's letter to the former Ohio State coach and certainly didn't know she had received a response.

The thought of the entire process, however, still brings a smile to Kramer's face. He had the letter framed and keeps it hanging on the wall of his basement office.

"My mother was a great Michigan fan, but she admired what Woody stood for," Kramer said. "She knew about all the players and coaches that she watched. She also knew the character of Woody and I guess she just wanted to show her appreciation."

While at Michigan, Kramer played against three Hayes'-coached teams (1954, 1955, and 1956). The two met briefly when

Hayes visited his good friend Vince Lombardi during preseason camps in Green Bay.

The friendship between Kramer and Hayes blossomed when Kramer served on the board of the Special Olympics for physically and mentally challenged children. Kramer invited Hayes to appear as a celebrity guest at a fund-raising banquet in what Hayes always referred to as "that state up north." Following the function, Kramer handed the coach a check for $1,500 as an honorarium.

"I handed him the check and he looked me square in the eye," Kramer recalled. "He said: 'I'm going to do one of two things with this check. I'm either going to tear it up or you can take it back and put it in the fund for the kids. I don't take money when it comes to these kids.'

"That's the kind of guy he was. After the dinner, all the kids came around him and really enjoyed talking to him. He wasn't that mean old ogre the press made him out to be. He was kind and gentle with a big heart for humanity."

Special Olympics is only one of countless charities with which Kramer has become involved.

"He's an easy mark because he can't say no," said Lew Price, who has known Kramer since childhood. "People who don't know Ron very well can be fractured by his rough exterior. But he's the kindest, most gentle human being I have ever met. When people try to talk about some of the things he's done for charity, he tries to scare them away. He doesn't talk. He just goes out and does things."

Dr. Keith Burch has been one of Kramer's physicians for more than thirty years. He also serves as one of the team physicians for the Detroit Lions.

"Of all the football players I've seen over the years, I've never seen one who's undergone more surgeries than Ron," Burch said. "It seems like almost every part of his body has been repaired or replaced.

"One part that never changes is the generosity of his heart. Ron comes across as being a little crazy, but I think that might be a little show. He's one of the most generous persons I've ever seen. He's always doing something for charity and people never know."

Kramer's affinity for helping charities probably emanated from his first hospital stay when he underwent knee surgery following his rookie season. During his rehab, he wandered the halls and witnessed kids being kept alive in iron lungs. He saw others recovering from surgeries far more serious than the one he had endured.

"It hit me," Kramer said. "Here I was hurt from playing a game of football and some of these kids were fighting for their lives."

He got involved with Special Olympics while playing for Green Bay. Not only did he commit his time and services, he also became an evangelical recruiter for anyone else who wanted to lend a hand.

Kramer was seeking a way to generate publicity for the charity. He invited Joe Falls to join him for the events to be held at Central Michigan University.

"I made it simple," Kramer said. "I told him I was taking him to see the greatest athletes I had ever seen."

Falls worked first for the *Detroit Free Press* and then the *Detroit News*. He spent a half-century in the profession and was revered as one of the nation's leading sports columnists.

"The experience changed my life," Falls said. "I could never thank Ron Kramer enough for having gotten me involved."

Before his death, Falls was instrumental in raising more than one hundred thousand dollars for the charity.

On the first day Falls visited one of the charity's functions, Kramer and he were watching a swimming event. One of the youngsters appeared to be struggling in the pool. Another, instinctively, jumped in to help.

Now it was Kramer's turn to get wet. Fully clothed, he dove into the water. Instead of grabbing the youngster who was struggling, he pulled the well-intentioned, would-be lifesaver out of the pool.

"That kid who was struggling wanted to finish," he explained. "He had to learn how to do it. No one was going to let him get hurt."

The kid did finish and the crowd exploded appreciatively as if watching a sudden-death touchdown pass in the Super Bowl.

"Joe just melted right on the spot," Kramer said. "There weren't too many dry eyes in the whole place … including mine."

Recruiting Falls to help the charity is a concrete example of what attorney and former University of Michigan Regent Neil Nielsen believes—that good people surround themselves with good people.

"Ron surrounds himself with friends of good quality," Nielsen said. "All one must do is to examine the cast of characters Ron recruits for the endless number of charities he supports. He's very sensitive. He empathizes. He shares the trials and tribulations of those around him. He can't refuse any charity. He's tireless."

At the dance following the competition, many of the participants asked the celebrity guests to accompany them onto the floor. Kramer says the entire experience is compelling.

"Let me tell you something," Kramer sounded like a Sunday morning evangelist. "I got more out of helping those kids than they ever got out of me. They were a blessing. That's what charity is all about."

Kramer's contributions to charities are diverse and thorough.

"A lot of us need help," he said. "If we've been blessed, then we have an obligation to share some of those blessings with those less fortunate. I know how fortunate I've been in my life."

One of the most amazing success stories involving Kramer's philanthropic zeal is the Walter Hagen Golf Tournament for the American Cancer Society. This was the celebrity golf tournament that helped to spawn a craze in the format and wandered far beyond the Michigan borders.

Former *Detroit Free Press* and *Detroit News* award-winning golf writer Jack Berry tagged the tournament as "the granddaddy of them all."

Kramer and Ken Janke, a well-respected financial CEO, cofounded the tournament in 1967.

"Ron was wise with his vision for the tournament," Janke said. "He wanted all proceeds to go to the American Cancer Society, but insisted on establishing the tournament as a separate charity so that we could call all the shots."

The results speak for themselves. In that first year, the tournament raised fifty thousand dollars. Now staged in twenty-seven states, the tournament raises about five million dollars annually in an effort to discover a cure for cancer.

In 1979, Kramer, Janke, and Detroit Lions Hall of Fame linebacker and former coach Joe Schmidt combined talents to establish the first NFL Alumni Golf Invitational for charity. Former and current NFL players, along with celebrities from other sports and professions, donate their time to generate funds. Half of the proceeds raised are designated for various children's charities. The other half helps former NFL players who find themselves in "dire financial need."

Again, the results speak for themselves.

Now each NFL Alumni Association around the country stages

such an event. Winners of each local event are invited to participate in the Super Bowl of Golf, staged in conjunction with the playing of the Super Bowl.

Kramer is known as an "easy mark" when it comes to donating time for such worthy fund-raising events. Each year, he and his core group of former Packer teammates attend six such tournaments in various cities in Wisconsin.

"The people of Wisconsin are beautiful," Kramer said. "You can't believe how much they love the Packers—the young guys and us old-timers, too."

Kramer participates in such tournaments as much for the camaraderie as he does for what he calls "giving something back."

"Any time I go to one of these things, I'm going to show the group I'm playing with a good time," he said. "If you make them laugh, those people who paid to play in the tournament are going to dig down into their pockets a little deeper. Why not show them a good time and help make the charity a few more bucks along the way? Besides ... what the hell's wrong with having a good laugh?"

Janke marvels at the enthusiasm Kramer still maintains for being in a position to help a friend in need.

"I could call him right now and say I need ten thousand dollars," Janke said. "He wouldn't ask what the money is for. He wouldn't ask me to sign any papers. And he may not even have the money. I promise you, though, somehow he would come up with it and be knocking on the front door. He acts rough and tough, but that's only a façade. I call him the 'Gentle Giant.'"

His gigantic efforts certainly have helped a significant number of charities now for more than forty years. And despite the aches and pains from a professional career resulting in eighteen surgeries, he's still the first one to arrive at each charity golf event.

That's just Kramer.

24 *When Team Meant Most*

Although life promises few guarantees, there are a handful of certainties that remain inevitable.

One of them is basic, like it or not. No matter how attached we become to anything of importance, time will change its presence. Perhaps its essence will remain untouched. But everything surrounding it is affected by society's shifting values.

Even the supposedly sacrosanct world of sports is not immune to such evolution. As a high-profile component of the American corporate community, change in sports is impossible to prevent. Sports no longer can be regarded simply as games. Once a mere blip on the radar screen of national economic health, sports now resonate with the thunder of a sonic boom.

Change alone does not make the games better. Nor does it make them worse. It simply makes one generation different from another and leaves it to fans to decide which is the best.

"It's so hard to compare athletes from different eras," Ron Kramer said. "For the most part, athletes today are bigger, stronger, and faster than when I played. They eat better food. They have better diets. They have better workout facilities. Each team has a roster full of specialty trainers and conditioning coaches. Nowadays a lot of the boys have personal trainers to work with all year round. We had one trainer and any off-season conditioning we did was on our own. Isn't it funny how we somehow managed to survive?"

The difference, of course, gets down to dollars. Many, many millions of dollars.

That comes as no surprise to the ticket-buying customers who sometimes have to pawn a treasured family heirloom to purchase a ticket to something like the Michigan/Ohio State football game or the World Series. The price of a Super Bowl ticket sometimes dictates a loan.

The endless spiral in ticket prices, concessions, corporate profits, and player salaries is fueled by the twin tower monsters of insatiable greed—television and marketing.

Kramer, arguably, was the best tight end ever to play the game. The most he earned in any single season was $37,000. He spent each off-season working what is considered to be an ordinary job, the same as every ticket-buying customer. His salary from the Packers wouldn't match that of today's lowest paid clubhouse attendant.

Certainly times and the economy have changed since Kramer was the scourge of every defensive back in the league. Those were the days when a loaf of bread cost a quarter and a new car loaded with every kind of gadget that glowed in the dark still could be bought for under $5,000.

Kramer feels he made a good living playing football. He adamantly supports that any player is entitled to squeeze every nickel out of an owner who is shrewd enough to pass any spike in the payroll on to the fans.

"God bless them all," he says. "I don't begrudge them. If the money is there and the players are entitled to it, then go out and get it. That's the American way."

Kramer merely believes that this passion for profit—larger than some countries' gross national product—by both ownership and players—has changed the game in subtle ways, and in some ways as subtle as a blindside quarterback sack.

Everything in life comes with a price. In this dollar-driven madness of big-time sports, the cost happens to be one of the inherent elements of the very essence of every game—teamwork.

"The concept of the team is being taken right out of sports," Kramer believes. "It's all become so individual because there's so much money going around."

Kramer quivers at the thought of the many lawyers, agents, and marketing madmen that often appear to be running the games.

"If you tried to fit them all into one stadium, you'd probably still have a waiting line a mile long outside the gates," he said.

Players are money-making commodities. They are tightly managed by handlers and agents who cleverly maneuver their clients to squeeze every possible dollar out of what appears to be a limitless marketing money pit.

"I'm not saying the players don't bust their butts," Kramer said.

"But do you ever notice how many wind up on the injured list? We used to hide our injuries so that none of the coaches knew. If you took yourself out of the lineup, there was no guarantee you'd ever make it back. If we didn't play every game of the season, there was no promise of a raise the following year. There wasn't even a promise of another year."

Television commercials don't look quite as sharp with a player endorsing some kind of product while nursing a broken hand with a black eye or scar across his face.

Even some of the rules have been changed to help prevent such unacceptable consequences.

Blocking and tackling have always been the heart and soul of football. The good teams do it better than the bad ones. It's the same today as it was seventy-five years ago.

The difference, however, is some of the essentials that were once part of those techniques are now restricted. Owners, of course, have their motives, too.

"We were taught to cross body block," Kramer said. "Get down low … hit the man hard … put your arm on him and make him roll. Now you can't do that anymore.

"Today you can't hit anyone in the head. You can't hit anyone low. You can't crack back on somebody. I understand that people can get hurt and players are a valuable piece of property. But isn't hitting part of the game? Is this really football?"

The number of franchises and the composition of each one also have affected the product on the field.

"When I broke into the league, there were only twelve teams," Kramer said.

Now there are thirty-four.

"We had thirty-two players, so everybody had to stay healthy," he continued.

Teams now carry fifty-three.

"We had four coaches," Kramer said. "Now you need a separate page in the program just to list all the coaches."

Kramer isn't complaining. His observations are simply impossible to dispute.

More than any single factor, television has done more to alter the course of football since the creation of the forward pass. Not only with its deep pockets, but also with technology that dissects every conceivable nuance of action like the sharpest scalpel slicing a dead frog in a biology lab.

When Kramer played for the Packers and Lions, all teams studied game films. Those films, for the most part, were shot from a single position. They lacked the intricately detailed panoramic scope of today's photographic technology.

"The technology today is incredible!" Kramer said. "There's replay, slow motion, stop action, isolation cameras, close-ups. They give you twenty different angles of the same play. It's fantastic for the fans and tremendous for a team preparing for the next game. A team scouting next week's opponent can zero in on tendencies of certain players like we never had a chance to do."

Of course, success still relies on execution.

"It always does," Kramer smiled. "That's why the Packers were so good."

Along with the benefits modern technology provides, there are some dangerous by-products. Players are aware of the impact of the camera's ubiquitous eye. They are keenly aware of the camera's power to turn a single play into a week-long highlight extravaganza.

It's impossible now to watch highlights of a game without at least one isolation of a player celebrating a touchdown by breaking into his personal interpretive dance in the end zone.

"What the hell is that all about?" Kramer shook his head. "We were always taught that a touchdown belonged to the whole team. It wasn't just the guy who caught the pass or the guy who threw it or the guy who ran the ball in. It was every member of the team that executed his assignment to make the play work. Do your dancing at night in a hall or some honky-tonk."

What would Lombardi have done if one of his players had danced in the end zone?

"See ya later, pal," Kramer laughed. "Act like you've been in the end zone before."

Gloves are another staple of the modern game that Kramer believes Lombardi would have scorned.

"Did you ever try to shave while wearing a glove?" Kramer asks. "It's the same thing as catching a football while wearing a glove on your hand. You just can't get the same feel."

When Kramer starred at Michigan, players still didn't wear facemasks on their helmets.

"That was one innovation that definitely had a positive impact," he chuckled.

The powerful images of television create universal ripples throughout the game at all levels. College players, high school players, even some of the Pop Warner kids league players emulate what they see the highly paid professionals do every Sunday on TV screens across America.

"Monkey see, monkey do," Kramer said. "Everything they see on their television they imitate on their fields."

Kramer is concerned about the direction of college football.

"Those young men aren't stupid," he said. "They see all the money that their schools are raking in from television. Why would a good young player want to play twelve or thirteen games a year for a scholarship when he can jump to the pros and make five million dollars a year? He can always go to school. The whole thing doesn't make sense."

Kramer feels the erosion of team unity is the ultimate result of so many changes.

"Lombardi always said that a guy like Henry Jordan played his position as well as Paul Hornung or anyone else on the field," Kramer said. "What he meant was that to be successful for any period of time, everyone has to perform as a team. That's what we're losing today. There are too many individuals."

Could teams from the past compete with those of today?

"Today's players are bigger, faster, and stronger," Kramer said. "Given the same conditions and equipment and all the other things, though, I'd like the Packers' chances. We played as a team and we lived as a team. Plus, we executed."

With the precision of a firing squad.

25 *The Gift of Friendship*

Barbara Kroflich's first encounter with Ron Kramer looked like a skit from *Saturday Night Live*.

It occurred shortly after Kramer had moved into his forested hideaway in Tyrone Hills, Michigan. Driving down the winding lane through the woods only a quarter of a mile from his home, en route to the Michigan/Ohio State football game in Ann Arbor, he made the sighting—an Ohio State flag flying from the Kroflich home.

Kramer stopped his truck and proceeded to the front door. He had no idea who lived in the house. It was, nonetheless, the perfect occasion on the perfect day for a little mischievous fun.

"Who's the Ohio Stater?" Kramer growled when Barbara answered the door.

Standing only a shade over five-feet tall and probably weighing a half less than Kramer, Barbara, naturally, felt only two steps away from panic. Her husband, Steve, happened to be away from home at the time.

"We're just from Ohio, that's all," Barbara tried to explain.

Kramer proceeded to acquaint her with the traditions of Michigan football without ever mentioning he happens to be a living tradition of the school himself. He topped his history lesson with a chorus of "Hail to the Victors."

Finishing his performance, he returned to his truck and proceeded to the game.

Months later, Kramer again was driving by the Kroflich home. This time Steve happened to be retrieving mail from the mailbox. Kramer stopped his truck.

"Do you live in that house?" Kramer asked.

Steve assumed his visitor was lost and was preparing to give him directions.

"Do you fly that Ohio State flag?" Kramer demanded.

Suddenly, it all made sense to Steve.

"You're the bully that frightened my wife half to death," Steve nearly shouted.

"And that's the ugliest damn hat in the world," he added in reference to the gold "M" on Kramer's blue baseball cap.

For some inexplicable reason, the two strangers broke into a smile. At the time the incident occurred, however, Barbara didn't see the humor in it.

"When I came home, her eyes were bulging like a bullfrog," Steve said. "She said some crazy Wolverine had just come down to threaten her."

Kramer explained the circumstances, stating that he couldn't resist the opportunity for a few laughs.

"I figured that," Steve replied, "but she was shaking."

Now Kramer and the Kroflichs are tighter than the Three Musketeers and laugh at the peculiarity of their meeting.

"He's the closest friend I ever had," Steve said of Kramer. "I never had a brother this close. If anyone tried to hurt that man, I'd have to kill him."

Originally from Bridgeport, Ohio, Steve remembers having seen Kramer play. However, neither Steve nor Barbara had a clue about the identity of their not quite so ordinary neighbor.

"Ron isn't the kind of guy who goes around telling people who he is," Steve said. "He just loves people. He enjoys having fun. He tries to act rough and tough like he's some kind of a bully. He's anything but. In fact, most people don't realize how gentle and generous Ron really is."

The Kroflichs and Kramer now spend considerable time together. They cook dinners for each other. They run errands for each other. There were times when Kramer was going through his divorce when he had a special date.

"Another prom night?" Steve would ask as he gave him the keys to his Cadillac to use for the evening.

They've grown so close now that neither feels the need to knock when visiting the other's home. And that led to another humorous incident that Barbara always will remember.

"My wife was washing dishes one time when she was only half-dressed," Steve recalled. "Kramer had something on his mind to tell me. He just walked straight through the kitchen without even looking at Barbara. I didn't know what was going on until I saw her running up the stairs. Now does that tell you how close we are?"

No football game, no championship, not even the pride he feels for his home means more to Kramer than a good friend. He considers them his most treasured rewards.

"I've been that way my whole life," Kramer said. "That's what life is all about. Good friends are the most precious gifts anyone can have."

The walls of Kramer's home are lined with framed photos of family and friends. It's his small way to stay close to the people who mean the most in his life. There are pictures of males and pictures of females.

"What difference does gender make?" he asks. "A friend is a friend. Even girlfriends you haven't seen in a long time still can be friends."

There are pictures of athletes and pictures of those who never wore a jock in their lives.

"What the hell does it matter what a person does for a living?" he asks. "Friendships don't come with restrictions."

There are pictures of those considered to be wealthy and pictures of those who carry lunch buckets to work.

"Who cares about money?" he asks. "There's no price tag on loyalty. The richest man in the world is poor if he doesn't have true friends."

One of Kramer's longtime friends is Jim Osborn, a Michigan State graduate and still diehard Spartan fan. Osborn is a retired ABC-TV executive who served as the Detroit affiliate's president and general manager from 1972 to 1979.

For the annual Michigan–Michigan State football battle, Kramer had a standing five-dollar wager.

"One of the dumbest things I ever did was to bet on Michigan State against Michigan," Osborn quipped. "But it was all for fun."

After one particularly tough Michigan State loss, Osborn filled an Aunt Jemima's syrup bottle with five hundred pennies to settle the wager.

"Do you have any idea how long it takes to squeeze five hundred pennies into a syrup bottle?" Osborn laughed. "But it was worth it."

Kramer still has the bottle as a reminder of his friend who now lives in San Francisco.

During the 1976 presidential campaign between Gerald Ford

and Jimmy Carter, Ford established a Detroit headquarters in an office down the hall from Osborn in the broadcast facility. On the day Mr. Ford arrived, Osborn allowed all three hundred-and-fifty employees to greet the sitting president on the lawn outside the facility. Osborn also invited Kramer and University of Michigan football coach Bo Schembechler and his wife Millie to join them.

After the president finished shaking hands with all of the station's employees, Kramer approached Mr. Ford.

"Hi, Mr. President," Kramer said with his usual candor. "I'm Ron Kramer."

The president, himself a former All-American for the Michigan Wolverines, smiled at his hulking fellow All-American.

"I know who you are," he chuckled.

Kramer then presented the president a new golf club and encouraged him to take a swing.

"I would have loved to have gotten him on the course for a friendly wager," Kramer cracked.

No man or woman needs international stature to become a friend of Kramer, however.

Tim Hudson is a millwright at a General Motors plant in Flint, Michigan. He lives on the other side of the dirt road that separates their houses. When he first met Kramer, he had no idea about his background.

"I'm a big football fan, but Ron was just a little before my time," he said. "That's the beautiful part about him, though. He doesn't go around bragging about all the things he's done. He's just a regular guy."

Hudson looks after Kramer's property when he's out of town. Hudson also uses the land to go bow hunting for deer.

"I've asked him to join me, but he won't go," Hudson said. "He absolutely won't kill anything. It's a small part of the real Ron Kramer that people don't see. He's really a gentle person who has general concern for people. The best part about Ron is his honesty. When he says something, he means it. He's a regular guy and a great friend."

Mike Yost's great uncle Fielding H. Yost, the accorded founding father of Michigan football tradition, died a couple of years before Mike was born. He met Kramer at a Michigan affair about fifteen years ago.

"It doesn't matter to Ron whose any relatives are," Yost said. "It doesn't matter what a person happens to do in life. If Ron accepts you for a friend, it's unconditional. And it lasts for life. Nothing matters more to Ron than friendship. He's always looking to do something for people. He's a great humanitarian. No one really knows how much work he does for charity. He's absolutely tireless."

Kramer has lived a charmed life. Few people have the opportunity to mingle with the world's greatest athletes, the most celebrated entertainers, and the most powerful captains of industry. Kramer has. He's even dined with Gerald Ford, former President of the United States.

While some of those personalities remain close, Kramer still treasures those special friends from childhood as much as the rich and famous he has picked up along the way.

Ron Klug has known Kramer since the second grade. They remain as tight today as they were more than sixty years ago.

"That's the way Ron is," Klug said. "Ron is just a regular guy who happened to be the best athlete almost anyone has seen. That's incidental to him when it comes to friendship. His loyalty and kindness are what set him apart. He never forgets a friend."

That's certainly the case with Bill Kehoe, a retired business executive from Royal Oak, Michigan. Kehoe delivered the newspaper to Kramer's home when his famous customer played for the Packers.

"After I finished my route, I used to stand in front of his house and kick the football or throw it up in the air hoping he would come outside," Kehoe recalled with a smile. "I remember the times he did, I was on cloud nine. He taught me how to catch the ball out in front of me and bring it into my body."

It must have worked because Kehoe wound up playing for his high school team and then for Ferris State University from which he graduated. The unlikely friendship matured after both became members of Royal Oak's Red Run Country Club.

"Ron is an enigma," Kehoe said. "He's very gruff on the outside, but such a giving person inside. His work for various charities is limitless. I have so many acquaintances, but few real friends. Ron is right up at the top of the list."

He must be. Why else would Kehoe have named his King Charles spaniel "Kramer?"

"I did it because both my dog and Ron make me smile," Kehoe explained. "I can't provide specifics, but just being around Ron makes a person smile. That's a very special gift."

Mari Monda Zdunic has her own reasons to smile about

her friendship with Kramer. Mari trains horses and operates a successful business teaching people to ride. She first met Kramer about twenty-five years ago and values not only their friendship, but also his philosophy about life.

"He's a friend and a mentor," she said. "When he becomes your friend, you can trust him with anything—professional or personal. He doesn't just talk. He's the kind of person who lives what he says."

Kramer had the opportunity to share his athletic expertise with a group of ladies taking lessons from Mari, and she still uses the experience as a teaching device today.

Kramer was returning home from one of his many trips to Ann Arbor when he decided to visit Mari. She was instructing about a half dozen ladies and was having trouble getting them to relax the pressure of their hands when holding the reins.

She asked Ron—as a former athlete—to share the importance of relaxation while still maintaining control. He began by telling them that catching a football in the middle of three defenders ready to knock a receiver's head from his shoulders demanded concentration and loose hands.

Then in typical Kramer fashion, he provided an analogy that made the advice perfectly clear.

"If you're going to masturbate, you have to keep your hands loose," he said.

"None of the ladies took offense," Mari said. "It made a bigger impression than anything I had said. I was trying to get them to relax and he accomplished it in ten seconds. They not only got the point, but they began laughing. Laughing dissipates tension, and when you're riding a thousand-pound horse, it's important to be relaxed. Ron's delivery is so human. His intelligence comes through."

Mari said she incorporates the story into her own teaching repertoire whenever the occasion arises.

"Ron is an accomplished athlete with a great sense of balance," Mari said. "He's also balanced in his approach toward life. He's able to step back and give people good advice."

Kramer's natural athletic ability makes him more than competent on the golf course. His competitive spirit makes him a tough opponent to beat.

Bob Rives is a successful St. Louis business executive who met

Kramer on the golf course. The two have been friends for more than twenty years. Rives remembers the meeting with a smile.

Rives was paired with Kramer in a friendly wager match against two other players. One of the opponents hit a drive into a patch of pine trees. As Kramer and Rives were riding toward the errant drive to help locate the shot, they noticed a ball trickling toward the fairway.

Calm, but with unmistakable firmness, Kramer asked the man what he lied.

"One," he meekly answered.

"Yeah," Kramer responded. "And that one is from behind the pine trees."

The man dropped his ball behind the trees and was preparing to shoot.

"Wait a minute," Kramer calmly said again as he walked toward the ball and unceremoniously stepped on it. "I'm not finished penalizing you."

Needless to say, there was no objection from the guilty party. Rives still smiles at the memory of Kramer's self-imposed justice regarding fair play.

After a friend's death, Kramer's loyalty is especially unshakable.

About twenty years ago, Kramer lost his good friend Brian Vidosh, a former athlete at Michigan State University.

"Ron was the first one there and really helped me make it through that terrible time," said Brian's widow, Linda. "In fact, I don't know how I would have made it without Ron. He took care of everything."

Not only did Kramer lend support at the moment, he also led in the establishment of the Brian Vidosh Scholarship Fund to Michigan State University.

When a friend is in trouble, Kramer is usually the first to call. When a particularly poignant problem struck Paul Hornung, Kramer, of course, was the first to call.

Hornung came under fire when the media misrepresented and then sensationalized an observation that he had made on a national radio broadcast regarding Notre Dame football recruiting policies.

Hornung suggested that his alma mater might have to adjust its academic standards in order to attract some of the better African-American athletes.

"Paul's not a racist," Kramer exploded. "Not by any stretch of the imagination. He respects and gets along with everybody. All he meant was that the school was going to have to make some adjustments in order to recruit some of the athletes that all the other powerhouses are getting."

When the media twisted the story into something it was not, Hornung found himself in the headlines for something that had never crossed his mind.

Kramer felt helpless for his friend, yet compelled to do something. He immediately called Jim Brandstatter and asked him to talk to his buddy. A former standout for the University of Michigan, Brandstatter serves as the radio voice for Michigan and Detroit Lions broadcasts.

"I told Ron all I can say is probably the same thing that you already told him," Brandstatter said. "Ron thought that maybe coming from someone in the media would have a little more punch."

Kramer called Hornung. Five minutes later, Brandstatter got the call from Kramer's friend.

Brandstatter explained to Hornung that a segment of the modern media survives on sensationalism. He advised Hornung that his best defense was to go on offense. He told him not to hide. He needed to address the situation himself to clarify the matter.

"I think any real sports fan knows that Paul Hornung is not a racist," Brandstatter said. "What impressed me is how quickly Kramer got involved. An injustice was happening to a friend and he was going to do whatever he could to help. That says everything about Ron Kramer. That tells you exactly what a friend means to him."

Ironically, Notre Dame seems to have adopted the very policy that Hornung had suggested.

There are times, in the world according to Kramer, when a friend is simply someone who can take a smash straight to the nose.

That's precisely what happened on an icy Green Bay evening outside of the King X restaurant and bar owned by Packer defensive back Jesse Whittenton. Kramer and Max McGee were inside celebrating something serious—perhaps another couple of inches of snow falling on the Green Bay sidewalks—when Hornung's date dashed frenziedly from the parking lot into the bar.

Hornung had gotten into a scuffle with a couple of inebriated customers who had made a derogatory remark after leaving the bar.

Hornung's temper flared and he punched one of the rowdies to the ground. The three were wrestling by the time Kramer charged through the door. Kramer picked all three up from the pile and held one of the attackers from behind to prevent him from making another move on Hornung.

When Hornung spotted him, he wound up and took a swing at the attacker's face. Unfortunately for Kramer, the hooligan ducked and Hornung's fist landed square on Kramer's nose.

"Ron said: 'Dammit, Hornung, I'm on your side,'" Hornung said.

Hornung had to laugh. So did Kramer.

"I told those two morons to get the hell out of there before I really got mad," Kramer said. "They took off running like scared rabbits and the fight was over. We went back inside for a few more cocktails and laughed our asses off. We still do today. That's what friends are for."

Mike Lucci didn't really get to know Kramer until the two became roommates when both played for the Detroit Lions. They've been best friends since. In 2003, after Lucci told Kramer he had been diagnosed with lymphoma, Kramer kept calling him to ask what he could do.

"Two, three times a day," Lucci laughed. "Finally I told him to give me a break. Three days later I called him. I asked him what was the matter ... don't you care about me anymore?

"Ron can be a little loud. Sometimes a little contentious. Underneath, though, he's a big softie. He really cares about people. When he's your friend, he's really your friend. There's no limit to his loyalty."

To the relief of Lucci, Kramer, and all concerned, the lymphoma is under control.

Dick Scott, a friend of Kramer's since high school, had a similar experience. A member of Scott's family had become seriously ill. Kramer hardly knew the person. Yet, after Scott asked Kramer to visit the patient to liven his spirit, Kramer took it six steps farther.

"Ron kept calling him just to make sure he was alright," Scott said. "He didn't have to do it, but that's the way he is. He has a heart of gold."

Scott added that Kramer visits at least once a month to give him relish, sweet pickles, apple sauce, salsa, or some concoction he's made at home.

"I would feel a great loss without those visits," Scott said. "The beautiful part about Ron is that the material things in life never meant anything to him. Friends mean everything."

Scott laughed before adding: "With two artificial hips and two artificial knees, though, I still can't figure out how he can dance with a martini on his head without spilling a drop."

Playing for the Packers was special for Kramer because it was a team comprised of unusual camaraderie.

"It's tough to explain because we remain just as close today as we were back then," he said. "It wasn't just with the guys. I have just as good a relationship with their wives and kids as anyone. Fuzzy's [Thurston] kids used to call me Uncle Ron. My kids used to call Hornung Uncle Paul. We see each other about a half dozen times each year and tell lies about how good we were. That closeness never changes. That's a tribute to Vince Lombardi."

Gary Knafelc always was amazed at Kramer's strength. He remains equally impressed with the softness that lies beneath Kramer's chest. Knafelc was the tight end who was replaced by Kramer.

A couple of years ago, Knafelc and his wife suffered the loss of their son. As soon as Kramer heard the news, he immediately called his predecessor to express his sympathy and ask if there was anything he could do.

"I knew it would be you to call first," Knafelc told him.

Kramer's concern for friends is certainly not predicated on celebrity.

John Apple lives a couple of miles from Kramer and is not a particularly avid sports fan. He is the retired treasurer of the operating engineers. He now owns a nursery that produces shade trees. The two met about twenty-five years ago when Apple had no idea of Kramer's famous football history.

Apple suffered a heart attack about five years ago. Unsurprising to Apple, Kramer was the first to call.

"He'd call or stop by just about every day," Apple said. "He always wanted to do something for me. That's the kind of pal he is. If you're in some kind of trouble, you don't ever wonder if he's covering your back. If you need something and he's got it, it's yours. Loyalty is a big thing with him."

Friendship to Kramer is a serious matter. It demands total commitment without any strings attached. For him, there are no limits to friendship.

As does Kramer, Hornung enjoys all the lifetime friends that came with playing for the Packers.

"Ron and McGee are special, though," Hornung said. "Since 1957, Ron and I have gone to the Kentucky Derby together forty-nine times. That ought to tell you something about how much we mean to each other."

Coming from a horse racing aficionado and a connoisseur of friendly wagering as is Hornung, that's quite a compliment.

Of course, Kramer is quite a not-so-ordinary friend.

26 *Underneath It All*

Barbara Giorgio and Ron Kramer met at a charity fund-raising event hosted by the Detroit Chapter of the National Football League's Alumni Association. Barbara was attending the event with six lady friends. Only one of the seven is a rabid football fan and it certainly wasn't Barbara. At the time, Barbara's knowledge of football was only that "it's a terribly vicious game."

Kramer was presented with a handsomely inscribed glass figurine saluting his dedication to raising funds for charity. During the evening, Kramer and Barbara had occasion to meet.

"One of my friends whispered to me: 'Do you know who that is?'" Barbara said. "I had no idea. I didn't know he had been a big star for the University of Michigan, then the Green Bay Packers and Detroit Lions."

Barbara told Kramer that his award looked quite distinctive.

"If you like it, take it," Kramer said as he handed her the figurine.

Not expecting such a response, she parried with another.

"If you want it back, you'll have to come and get it," she said.

Before the evening ended, Kramer asked if he could call her. One week later he did. The two have been dating since and make a handsome couple, even though some of their perspectives are as diverse as those espoused by George Bush and John Kerry.

Barbara had never before met a man who had made a living in the unconventional life of professional football. Taking it a step further, in fact, she had never met anyone as unconventional as Kramer.

"To say he's different doesn't do justice to the word," Barbara said. "He's not a man of opinions. He's a man of convictions. Some of them are a bit bizarre, but he stands by them."

Barbara admires the strength of his convictions, even though sometimes she disagrees with the underlying premise.

For instance, he once drove straight to her house following a University of Michigan football game wearing jeans and a yellow T-shirt. They had planned to visit the house of one of Barbara's sons for a reunion with a visiting old friend. The affair was informal, but Barbara noticed a stain down the back of Kramer's shirt. Someone had inadvertently spilled a glass of wine on him at one of the tailgate parties.

Barbara wanted Kramer to wear a different shirt. He couldn't understand the cause for her concern.

"What's the difference?" he asked. "The stain is on the back."

Barbara pulled a new golf shirt that Kramer had given her from the drawer. It was unworn and extra large. Reluctantly accommodating, he put it on.

"He refuses to compromise his convictions," she said. "But there are times when he'll find a way to change so that those convictions aren't violated."

In August 2006, Kramer and Barbara decided to celebrate both of their birthdays with a cruise to Alaska. Before leaving, however, Kramer emphatically stated he would not wear a necktie on the trip. How could any man, he reasoned, truly enjoy a vacation with a tie strung around his neck?

Barbara informed him that she was going to wear an appropriate evening gown to the formal dinner of the cruise. She later placed a new shirt and necktie on his pillow and said if he didn't choose to dress properly he could eat dinner alone at one of the ship's delis and the two could meet afterward.

The pair made a spectacular couple at the dinner table.

Perhaps the most stunning aberration of Barbara's wardrobe proprieties occurred one late summer afternoon when she, Kramer, and good neighbors Steve and Barbara Kroflich decided to go for a fish fry dinner at one of the most popular restaurants near Kramer's home.

Kramer was already at his truck by the time the rest of the party was getting ready to leave the house.

"Let's go, I'm waiting," Kramer shouted into the house.

When Barbara got to the door, she saw that he was wearing the same white T-shirt and bathing suit that he had worn during the afternoon. She looked incredulously aghast at the other Barbara.

"Don't worry, honey," the other Barbara said. "He does that all the time."

Barbara is learning, of course, that Kramer's interpretation of life operates on a totally different frequency than the rest of the world. Barbara has become well aware of Kramer's gruff and sometimes coarse exterior. She also is genuinely moved by the sensitive character that lives inside his heart.

"He's so much more sensitive than he lets on to be," she said. "Without question, he is the most generous person I have ever gone out with. He loves to order things off the television. When he does, he'll order one for himself and one for me. He'll bring it over and without making a big scene, he'll just say: 'I know you'd love this.' Some people may not realize what a thoughtful, caring person he really is."

Perhaps even more touching are simple greeting cards that he often delivers in person.

"Rarely does he show up without some little gift or card," she said. "It may not be anything big; it's the thought behind it. He's an extremely giving person."

The stark contrast between that giving person and the profession from which he came still bewilders Barbara.

"Football is such a violent game," she said. "People banging heads and running into each other. I don't like any kind of physical violence. He's had so many surgeries. How he walks and how he moves now is painful to watch. He's amazing, though. You never hear one word of complaint from him. He has a gift for accepting life and moving on."

Barbara is a wise lady to understand that family and friends mean more to Kramer than any of life's material matters.

"They mean everything to him," she said. "He absolutely adores his son Kurt and daughter Cassie and his grandchildren. He has so many good friends, especially the men he played with at Green Bay."

Barbara has accompanied Kramer for several functions and reunions in Green Bay.

"Some of the guys will come up and tease me by asking if I'm still hanging out with him," she smiled. "I can tell when these guys get together how much it means to them. They hug each other and kiss each other. It must be a special kind of camaraderie."

Barbara also is impressed by some of the things that don't matter as much to Kramer as they do to others.

"He doesn't care about money," she said. "If he did, he'd sell his house and property and put condos up around the lake. He spends like crazy. He enjoys each day. If he spends every dime, he knows his kids will have a nest egg with the property."

Sometimes Kramer's generosity to strangers even surprises Barbara. At a popular Ann Arbor restaurant before being seated, Kramer and Barbara met a young couple waiting for a table. Each happened to be a nuclear scientist employed by the University of Michigan. Kramer invited them to sit in his booth.

"Ron paid for the whole thing," Barbara said. "He had never seen them before in his life. He would take a billionaire to dinner and fight to pay the tab."

Perhaps not quite billionaires, Kramer has taken Barbara into the homes of various influential families.

"One of the beautiful things about Ron is that he has friends from every walk of life," Barbara said. "Some are quite wealthy, but he's totally unfazed by money. Ron measures the man by how good a person he is. Money doesn't matter. It's all about loyalty and trust."

Barbara smiled when asked about Kramer's hidden hideaway that he calls home.

"Would I invite a lot of people to his house?" she smiled. "No. But my son and son-in-law absolutely love it. All men do. They call it a man's heaven of sports memorabilia. It's hard to understand, though, how anyone can have a Lladro vase sitting in the corner of the room with a Beanie Baby stuck inside."

Maybe because that's just Kramer?

"Ron finds contentment in that house," she said. "He's not a conformist. He's totally free. He's gregarious, but he fits the description of being introverted. The true meaning of an introvert is someone who recharges within himself. He likes to be around people, but he loves being home. He values truth above everything else. He's far more sensitive than people realize."

Despite the stark disparity in their approach to finding contentment, Barbara believes that there are similarities between herself and Kramer.

"We're a lot the same, but express it differently," she observed. "I wish one day he'd learn to express his feelings. I think he doesn't want to appear to be vulnerable. He doesn't express his feelings about traumatic stuff. Ron is more of a doer than a talker."

Despite those dissimilarities, Barbara appreciates the kindness, warmth, and honesty that Kramer never fails to display.

"He is honest," Barbara said. "He can be cynical about a lot of things going on in the world, but he's never critical about friends."

Kramer's interest in Barbara must be as deep as the one she has in him. How else could anyone explain his patience with giving her a crash course in the fundamentals of football?

"I knew absolutely nothing about football," she said. "So he's drawn up charts and diagrams to show me how each position is supposed to work. When we watch a game on TV, he becomes so intolerant of what the announcers say. He doesn't think they know what they're talking about. He absolutely hates when players dance around in the end zone after scoring a touchdown. I think it's funny when they do it."

So there are differences between Kramer and Barbara. But those differences merely reinforce the relationship that Kramer has come to appreciate.

"This is the first time in my life that I've gone with a woman that's near my age," Kramer cracked.

It's the first time Barbara has ever existed in a world as unconventional as the one in which Kramer thrives.

"One thing for sure," Barbara said. "It's not the type of relationship that could ever get boring."

One never is with Kramer involved.

27 *Challenge and Contentment*

At about eight o'clock on the evening of January 3, 2007, Ron Kramer "just didn't feel right."

For a couple of months, he had experienced discomfort in his chest. The previous April, he needed two stents to be inserted into an artery leading to his heart. Maybe, he figured, the discomfort had something to do with that.

The pain on that particular evening, however, felt different. Kramer called his loyal neighbor Steve Kroflich, who told his friend he would be over in five minutes.

"It seemed like I just hung up the phone and there he was, walking though my door," Kramer laughed. "He's a Nervous Nelly. I told him Superman doesn't move that fast. I was still putting on my socks."

Kramer and Kroflich piled into the car for the ride to nearby Genesys Regional Medical Center.

About thirty people were in the Emergency Room lobby when Kramer casually mentioned to a member of the hospital staff that he was having chest pains. The lady quickly plopped Kramer into a wheelchair, and Steve Kroflich rolled him into the Emergency Room, where another member of the staff who had treated him previously immediately noticed him.

"Kramer," he said. "How are you doing? Too bad about Michigan in the Rose Bowl."

The two talked about the game for a few moments before Kramer looked at his friend Kroflich. "I'm gonna pass out," Kramer said.

"I went boink ... completely out."

It was the last thing Kramer remembered until waking up

to see about twenty faces staring down at him as they frantically scurried to revive him.

While he was unconscious, the E.R. staff administered electrical defibrillator treatment, along with an old-fashioned chest pounding procedure to prevent Kramer from slipping into permanent "boinkness."

"When I woke up, I saw all these people," Kramer said. "A few were sticking needles into me. Another was pinching me. One was doing this ... one was doing that."

Kramer tried to get his focus.

"What the hell is going on?" he asked.

"You just had a cardiac arrest," a voice answered.

"What does that mean?" Kramer asked.

"It means you almost didn't make it," the voice responded.

Three days and two more stents later, Kramer was released from the hospital.

"St. Peter wouldn't let me through the gates," Kramer joked with his friends. "I guess in football, this would be called a play-off game. The Super Bowl is the one you don't come back from."

Kramer's outwardly carefree demeanor is merely part of the total package. Underneath, he appreciates how fortunate he was.

"I was lucky," he said. "If we had left the house ten minutes later, I might have had this thing in the car. Then Steve and I both would have been dead because he probably would have run into a tree."

Kramer particularly appreciates the care, concern, and professionalism of the entire Genesys Hospital staff that combined to save his life.

"I'm extremely grateful," Kramer said. "But I'm not going to worry about what happened. It's done. That game's been played. I've got another one to play today. Let's get on with it."

Kramer's voracious appetite for life remains unshakable. The concern expressed by family and friends, however, moved him more than any attacking linebacker ever could.

The calls from Kurt and Dawn (son and daughter-in-law) and Cassie and Brian (daughter and son-in-law) were precious. So were those from his grandchildren and sister, Anna Marie.

"Barbara was super with the way she took care of me," Kramer said.

Calls from former teammates and friends across the country particularly impressed Kramer about how truly blessed he is.

"Family and friends," Kramer said with the pride of a new father. "Nothing has meant more to me in my whole life. So I had a little setback, but the whole team stuck together."

That means more to Kramer than anything else in the world. The incident—though scary—helped to define Kramer's self-acceptance.

Bob Dylan's vision of success captures the essence of Kramer like a digital snapshot.

"What's money?" the iconic songwriter, singer, and poet once asked. "A man is a success if he gets up in the morning and goes to bed at night and in the middle does what he wants to do."

That may not reflect the popular perception of the American Dream, but it sure makes the burden of success sound a whole lot more appealing.

Kramer gets the message. He's managed to live the philosophy his entire life. Now that he's reached a point that hardly any professional athlete believes will ever arrive, he takes tremendous satisfaction in the fact that true contentment comes without the glare of the limelight or any kind of media hoopla.

"Dad is content," said son Kurt. "It's not a phony kind of contentment. He is really growing into the regular guy that he is."

That sounds so simple, but can be such an excruciatingly painful journey in the life of one considered to be a living sports legend.

American society stops one step short of apotheosizing those rare physical specimens that can dominate all the games through which so many sports fanatics vicariously live. Even a legitimately anointed saint might have trouble refuting the self-centered importance an icon like that must feel with people tripping over their own feet trying to ingratiate themselves.

"People can't understand how someone like him gets conditioned to a certain lifestyle," Kurt said. "At seventeen years old, he was sought by every major college in the country to honor a particular university with his presence. When he was a professional star, people were begging him to allow them to do him favors."

Sounds like a fairy tale life. Fairy tales, of course, are only make-believe. Living happily ever after is a finish that must be self-attained.

"Kids don't really know their parents," Kurt reasoned. "When I was a kid, I just knew Dad as Ron Kramer—big-time football player that everyone wanted to be around."

Now Kurt views him with a completely different perspective. And he's grateful for the man he sees.

"I've always been proud of Dad, but now it's for different reasons," Kurt said. "I didn't know what the real person is. Now I do, and I love him so dearly."

Daughter Cassie shares her brother's happiness.

"I feel content that Dad's in a good place," Cassie said. "He's happy, busy, and so much more accepting of life. He's a lot more at peace and enjoys everything and everyone around him. There's a lot less pressure to perform at a certain level that everyone just sort of expected from him."

Kramer still attacks each day with the same vigor he used to attack enemy linebackers ... or even teammate Ray Nitschke in Vince Lombardi's dreaded nutcracker drill.

He simply does it in a more wizened way.

"He's discovered that just being Ron instead of the famous Ron Kramer can be a pretty neat thing," Kurt said. "He's not concerned so much with being Ron Kramer as opposed to being plain old Ron. There's a different group of people who are interested in being with Ron more than they are with Ron Kramer. Friendships are truer."

That, of course, does not negate the real friendships that Kramer still maintains with former teammates. Those Green Bay Packers teams under Lombardi created a special brotherhood. Those football wars in which they battled triumphantly, shoulder-to-shoulder, created lifetime bonds that the average fan can never quite appreciate.

Kramer relishes the opportunity for the half dozen annual trips he makes to Green Bay for charity fund-raising functions that only this special collection of champions can share. The camaraderie that exists between members of one of sports' true dynasties is more meaningful than any pension the NFL can offer.

Kramer is just as quick to donate his time in support of local charities within the state of Michigan.

"Ron has never forgotten where he came from," said Ron Klug, a friend since the two were in the second grade. "Ron has been privileged to meet a lot of famous people. But he gets just as much satisfaction being with people he's known all his life as he does with those people with the fancy reputations."

Kurt always felt his father's affinity toward regular people.

"Dad has always loved regular people," Kurt said. "When someone came up to him and said, 'I'm from East Detroit and I know your mother,' he'd drop everything and do whatever that person asked for."

There was a time, no doubt, when Kramer would have squirmed at the thought of simply spending time in the serenity of his hideaway home. Now he savors it sweetly as he once did strapping on the pads.

He thoroughly enjoys critiquing football games on his wide-screen TV. He becomes engrossed—sometimes to the point of being vocal—when watching political programs. He has grown particularly enamored with history shows and those dealing with animals and nature. It helps him to better appreciate all of the critters with which he shares his 115 acres of solitude.

The pictures that line his walls provide a visual link with the good friends he's made along the way.

He emphatically chooses to live in the present, however. Pictures from his celebrated football career at the University of Michigan and particularly from the Green Bay Packers are merely appreciated, not tickets to the past.

"I don't need to be reminded about how good we were," he says with tasteful nonchalance. "We knew we were good. Nobody has to tell us."

Kurt appreciates his father's sense of contentment in his uniquely comfortable home. Kramer maintains that any guy who had the chance to live where he does would do so in a minute.

"He loves to look at all the stuff on the walls," Kurt said. "The amazing thing is that there are very few purchased items. They are things that people have given him over the years. Some things are a little strange. Who else would have a Brett Favre beanie doll stuffed into a fifteen hundred-dollar vase?

"But that's alright. He says the house might be a little cluttered, but it's exactly the way he wants it. Dad will die in that house."

In the meantime, however, there's a lot of living to do. A whole lot.

Kurt enjoys his frequent visits to his father's home where the two find meaningful satisfaction merely strolling through the woods. Sometimes they just sit at the edge of the dock idly casting a fly rod while they leisurely talk.

"He's easier to be around now," Kurt said. "He's always been fun, but he used to be so dominant. Now he knows he doesn't have to try."

Concrete evidence of Kurt's observation was his father's 2006 summer cruise to Alaska with lady friend Barbara.

"It used to be a case of 'Here's what I'm doing and if you want to come along, fine,'" Kurt said. "Now he seems to be doing more stuff that other people want.

"Dad and Barbara seem to be good for each other. He treats her with a level of respect that I'm happy to see. She is bright and very socially correct. She's direct with him and tells Dad what she thinks, but does so privately."

Cassie is happy about her brother's relationship with her father, albeit a trifle envious.

"It makes me a little jealous because they have that special father/son relationship," she said. "I do feel happy, though, because it's so good for both of them. Dad has settled down a lot and is so enjoyable to talk with. He's a lot more willing to listen to people and a little more open-minded. He's got great business sense and is a good mentor for Kurt."

More than anything else, Cassie is profoundly proud of her father's intense sense of family.

"He's a tremendous grandfather and truly loves being one," she said.

From the streets of East Detroit to the halls of the University of Michigan. From the frozen field of Green Bay's Lambeau Field to the stature of being called one of the National Football League's all-time greatest tight ends.

Ron Kramer, without doubt, is one of twentieth-century America's all-time purest athletes. Now he's discovering that merely being Ron can be just as fulfilling.

"He's fully enjoyed the journey and isn't worried about the destination," Kurt said.

Now it's Kramer's turn to agree with his young wise son.

"I love where I am in life," Kramer claims with the exuberance of a raw rookie. "I wouldn't want to be any other age. I already went through the past. I know who I was and what I did. I'm enjoying the challenges I face now."

Of course, what else could be expected of one so gifted that the footprints he left in his profession will last forever regardless how much the game changes?

All-American. All Pro. And all the while, living life to its fullest.

That's just Kramer.

Works Cited

Hornung, Paul. *Golden Boy.* New York: Simon & Schuster, 2004.

Izenberg, Terry, Director and writer. *A Man Named Lombardi.* Narrator George C. Scott, Gould Entertainment Corporation Presentation, 1978.

Lombardi Jr., Vince. *What It Takes to Be #1.* New York: McGraw-Hill, 2001.

Maraniss, David. *When Pride Still Mattered.* New York: Simon & Schuster, 1999.